D0109821

WHAT WILL YOUR TOMBSTONE SAY?

Revised and Updated Edition

**52 Short Essays on
Spirit-Filled Church,
Spirit-Led Ministry, and
Spirit-Empowered Discipleship**

Thomson K. Mathew

What Will Your Tombstone Say?
Revised and Updated Edition

Copyright © 2018 by Thomson K. Mathew
www.thomsonkmathew.com

All rights reserved. No portion of this book may be reproduced, stored in a retrieval system, or transmitted in any form or by any means—electronic, mechanical, photocopy, recording, scanning, or other—except for brief quotation in critical reviews or articles, without the prior written permission of the author.

Published by:
GOODNEWS BOOKS
Kottayam, Kerala 686 004, India

Unless otherwise indicated, Scripture quotations are taken from the New King James Version ®, Copyright © 1982 by Thomas Nelson. Used by permission. All rights reserved.

Scripture verses marked KJV are taken from the Holy Bible, King James Version (public domain).

Scripture quotations marked MSG are taken from *The Message* (MSG) Copyright © 1993, 1994, 1995, 1996, 2000, 2001, 2002 by Eugene H. Peterson.

Scripture quotations marked NASB are taken from the New American Standard Bible (NASB)
Copyright © 1960, 1962, 1963, 1968, 1971, 1972, 1973, 1975, 1977, 1995 by The Lockman Foundation.

Scripture quotations marked NIV are taken from the Holy Bible, New International Version®, NIV® Copyright © 1973, 1978, 1984, 2011 by Biblica, Inc. ®
Used by permission. All rights reserved worldwide.

ISBN: 978-1-9851-7887-8

Global version printed by:
CreateSpace
An Amazon Company

In honor of
my grandparents and parents and
my wife's grandparents and parents, who
lived by faith and labored as pioneer Pentecostals
in the hard soil of India.

CONTENTS

FOREWORD

Wisdom literature provides advice to people to help them deal successfully with the practical affairs of everyday life and to instruct them to handle life's issues through short stories, parables, pithy sayings, and wise maxims. This literature was written down to preserve the oral traditions and to make this practical wisdom available for future generations. It was designed to teach wisdom, to develop character, and to encourage a committed relationship with the Lord.

In his revised and updated edition of *What Will Your Tombstone Say?* Thomson K. Mathew provides wise counsel, practical theology, pastoral care insights, and devotional inspiration. In this collection of fifty-two essays, Mathew sets forth three topics about which he is impassioned: Spirit-filled church, Spirit-led ministry, and Spirit-empowered discipleship. He emphasizes the importance of the Holy Spirit and His empowering presence for twenty-first-century church leaders, ministers, missionaries, educators, and followers of Christ.

Mathew's anthology contains wisdom teachings such as those found in Proverbs and in the Gospels. Jesus used common, everyday events that would be familiar to His audience to teach profound truths. The articles and essays found in this collection likewise convey simple truths in a unique and practical way with a depth of understanding and wisdom gleaned from the memory of the author's former days in the East and his current daily life in the West.

The title of this anthology betrays the author's hope that through this book readers will be challenged to fulfill God's purpose in their lives as written in Ephesians 2:10 (NIV): "For we are God's handiwork, created in Christ Jesus to do good works, which God prepared in advance for us to do." Mathew is an outstanding example of a man of God who is successfully fulfilling God's purpose in his life. He truly practices what he preaches. He is an excellent communicator of sound biblical and theological teachings and practical wisdom. He has extensive experience as a pastor, chaplain, seminary professor of pastoral care, and a former dean of a well-known Pentecostal/charismatic seminary. He is also a devoted husband, father, grandfather, colleague, and friend, and a conference speaker at home and abroad.

The articles and essays in this collection will instruct, enlighten, provoke thought, and encourage God's people to follow Jesus Christ's example of proclaiming the good news through Spirit-empowered teaching, preaching, and healing as recorded in Matthew 9:35 (NIV): "Jesus went through all the towns and villages, teaching in their synagogues, proclaiming the good news of the kingdom and healing every disease and sickness." Jesus' ministry was empowered by the Spirit: "God anointed Jesus of Nazareth with the Holy Spirit and power, and . . . he went around doing good and healing all who were under the power of the devil, because God was with him" (Acts 10:38 NIV). The insightful nuggets of wisdom in *What Will Your Tombstone Say?* will inspire people to partner with the Holy Spirit in their personal lives and in their respective ministries, and they will also provide instruction and helpful tools for the followers of Jesus Christ to enable them to fulfill the sacred commission of bringing His healing message of salvation and restoration to this generation.

Cheryl L. Iverson, PhD
Professor and Former Associate Dean
College of Theology and Ministry
Oral Roberts University

INTRODUCTION

This is a collection of articles and essays on three of my favorite topics: Spirit-filled church, Spirit-led ministry, and Spirit-empowered discipleship. These articles of varying lengths, written at different stages of my service as a minister, reflect my understanding of these topics, and observations, concerns, and recommendations regarding them based on my experience as a pastor, hospital chaplain, theological educator, and seminary dean.

The first edition of *What Will Your Tombstone Say?* was published to make this material available to my students. I have revised the original volume and updated it by replacing a number of items with articles and essays I have written more recently. I hope these pages written in simple vocabulary will reach beyond the classroom.

I was born and raised in a pastor's home in South India, but lived most of my life in America. My father and grandfather were both Pentecostal preachers in India. My grandparents were Saint Thomas Christians who became Pentecostals. The fact that I grew up in Pentecostal parsonages in India has influenced my writings.

My life in the West is the prism through which I have been looking at topics covered in this collection. My life as a pastor, my clinical training and work as a chaplain, my experiences as a husband and father, my work as a professor of pastoral care and dean, and my life as a preacher at churches and conferences is reflected in these pages. Although I am a third-generation Pentecostal, my perspective is not necessarily based on any particular denomination. I belong to so many worlds by virtue of my being a preacher, immigrant, and a teacher at an interdenominational charismatic seminary.

Basically, I am a modern pilgrim. Pilgrims are not defined by the country through which they travel, but by the land of destination. In a sense everyone in today's world is an immigrant, a resident alien, in that all of us live now in a world different from the one in which we were born, but all of us who follow Christ are called to be pilgrims. Life by faith is a pilgrimage. The book of Hebrews, chapter 11, is a list of pilgrims. Abraham, who is prominent in this chapter, looked for a city whose builder and maker is God. We are to follow his example. In these pages, you will see a modern pilgrim's perspective on matters of faith and life.

These writings cover a lot of territory. I write about the church, ministry, and discipleship. I write about wholeness and holiness. I write as a minister of the gospel and trainer of ministers. I write as a preacher of the Word and teacher of seminarians, but I am addressing not just ministers or ministerial students. These articles and essays have been written for general Christian readership.

I am indebted to the many teachers, preachers, and writers who have impacted my life and who reveal themselves between these lines. I am forever grateful to my colleagues at Oral Roberts University College of Theology and Ministry who keep me engaged in theological discussions. I wish to express my thanks to my beloved wife, Molly, GOODNEWS BOOKS chief editor C. V. Mathew, and editorial assistant Marlene Mankins.

I am grateful for the opportunity to share this collection, and hope that readers will find in these pages some useful information and a few insights. If someone finds a word of encouragement or a moment of inspiration as a result of reading these pages, I would be more than grateful.

—Thomson K. Mathew
College of Theology and Ministry
Oral Roberts University
7777 S. Lewis Avenue
Tulsa, Oklahoma 74171
USA

www.thomsonkmathew.com

PART I

SPIRIT-FILLED CHURCH

1

A SPIRIT-FILLED CHURCH

Being a Spirit-filled church has very little to do with the denomination to which it may belong. I have seen non-Pentecostal Pentecostal churches and Pentecostal non-Pentecostal churches in more than one nation. To me, a contemporary Spirit-filled church is one that reflects in a twenty-first-century way the life, leadership, and ministries of the earliest church described in the book of Acts.

A Spirit-filled church is a community of believers who are open to the active and dynamic presence of the Holy Spirit. These believers do not quench the Spirit, but welcome the presence, power, and manifestations of the Holy Spirit among them, always expressing themselves decently and in order.

A Spirit-filled church is a group of people who recognize the supernatural gifts of the Holy Spirit along with the leadership gifts called the apostles, prophets, evangelists, pastors, and teachers. The leaders make sure that the life of the church is nurtured and that worship practices are conducted in an orderly fashion. In this way, they equip the saints for the work of the ministry (Eph. 4:10).

A Spirit-filled church gives priority to preaching and teaching of the Word of God. Spiritual feeding of its members is a major concern of the leadership, which includes some individuals who are fully devoted to the ministry of the Word (see Acts 6:2).

The mission of the Spirit-filled church is discipleship and spiritual formation of its members for the fulfillment of God's purposes in the world. Commitment to this mission causes the church to function as if its ultimate purpose is the development of new ministers. The purpose of ministry, then, is to develop ministries and ministers.

A Spirit-filled church is a caring church. Members break bread together, learn the Word together, fellowship with one another, and share their means with those in need, especially those within the household of faith (Acts 2: 42; Gal. 6:10).

A Spirit-filled church attempts to keep a favorable relationship with the community around it, even when that community is resistant to its mission and even its very existence. It respects authority and appeals to authority within the community when appropriate.

A Spirit-filled church is a worshipping community. This community gathers regularly to worship God with psalms, hymns, and spiritual songs, making melody in each heart (Eph. 5:19).

A Spirit-filled church is a community of hope. Its members maintain a concurrently finite and transfinite (eternal) view of life. Relationships and priorities are evaluated in light of their eternal significance. The line between secular and spiritual is thin, and temporal things are never the top priority.

A Spirit-filled church is a growing community, growing both in size and in depth. Through the preaching of the Word and faithful testimony of each believer, the church grows and goes from addition to multiplication (Acts 2:47). A Spirit-filled church is an organization and a living, dynamic organism at the same time, loved by God, redeemed by the blood of Jesus Christ, and empowered by the Holy Spirit.

2

WHAT DOES A HEALTHY
CHURCH LOOK LIKE?

Modern Americans are increasingly concerned about their health. Billions of dollars are spent on improving people's health and well-being, but in spite of this and the availability of the most advanced technology in the world, our national worry about health issues continues.

While people worry about their physical health, often they neglect their mental and spiritual health. Physicians say that a lot of our physical symptoms are rooted in psychological problems. Psychologists, on the other hand, say that much of our psychological problems can be traced to the dysfunctional families from which we came or in which we now live. Preachers often laugh at this suggestion, but family therapists spend a considerable amount of time and money doing research on improving the health of families. Published studies show that we can learn much from their research about maintaining healthy families.

The Church of Jesus Church is more than an organization; it is a living organism. All living organisms must grow, develop, and maintain their health. But what does a healthy church look like?

Pastoral theologian Charles V. Gerkin has written on the subject of Christian congregations. In his book *An Introduction to Pastoral Care*, Gerkin examines the congregation as a community of faith and describes five characteristics of a healthy congregation.[1] I believe all churches will benefit from examining themselves in light of these characteristics.

First of all, according to Gerkin, a healthy congregation is a community of language. Second, a healthy congregation is a community of memory. Third, a healthy congregation is a community of inquiry. Fourth, a healthy congregation is a community of mutual care. Finally, a healthy congregation is a community of mission. So, a healthy church must be a Christ-centered community of language, memory, inquiry, mutual care, and mission.

1. A Community of Language

By the term *a community of language*, Gerkin is not talking about any particular native language. He is talking about the language of the Bible and the images and metaphors contained in the Bible. According to Gerkin, we must become a community that uses biblical language, images, and metaphors. We must see the Word of God forming and informing our worldview.

The Bible is the history of a people called by God to follow Him. It contains the history of the people of God in migration as well as in exile. Migration and exile are two different things.

---

1 Charles V. Gerkin, *An Introduction to Pastoral Care* (Nashville: Abingdon, 1997), 122–28

Exiles are forced to live the way they do. Migrants are volunteers. America is a nation of immigrants. Modern Americans are migrants, and they are coexisting with a small number of true natives. According to the biblical language, we must all see ourselves as aliens and pilgrims in this world, looking for a city whose builder and maker is God (Heb. 11:13; 1 Peter 2:11).

2. A Community of Memory

A community of memory is one that remembers its past, especially the ways in which the Lord has brought it thus far. We are told not to forget all His benefits (Ps. 103:2). It offends God when His people forget His mercies.

We must not forget our past and what the Lord has done for us. Moreover, we should teach our children about our past, lest they forget their roots. This means that we must find ways to keep the memory of God's dealings with us alive. We need preachers and teachers who can remind us of our past, as well as take us to a better future.

3. A Community of Inquiry

Charismatic students often tell me how their own communities do not encourage them to continue their education. This is true especially of those who study theology and ministry. Somehow we think that only young people should be learners. We are ignoring the fact that the whole world is moving to the concept of lifelong learning. This is especially true in North America. All major corporations are supporting their employees in their quest for lifelong learning. The world is changing so fast and new information is generated so rapidly that unless one remains a student for life, it is impossible to excel in one's field. The old Sunday-school-is-for-kids mentality must change in our churches. Being ignorant does not glorify God.

The average adult in America changes jobs several times within a lifetime. Student days cannot be limited to young adulthood. There are so many user-friendly ways adults can learn now. We must take advantage of these. Typical seminary students in North America are in their thirties. We must not discourage adult learners. Learning is the best form of investment.

We must get beyond the fear of education. We must become an inquiring community—inquiring about the profitable things of this world and the things of God.

4. A Community of Mutual Care

The church must become a truly caring community. Being so caught up in seeking our own well-being, we tend to neglect the needs of others. To ensure a good future for all of us, we must find ways to care for one another. Let us seek the kingdom of God—the well-being of others in the name of Christ—first. God has promised that as we seek His kingdom, all the other things we need shall be added to us (Matt. 6:33).

Many churches are growing but are not providing enough mutual caring for their members. A healthy church is a caring community. We must all become caregivers by being trained to assist others who are struggling with various challenges.

5. A Community of Mission

Christians in America need a missions strategy that is bigger than themselves. We have been too shortsighted in our missionary strategy. Short-term missions are definitely in God's plan. However, we should not assume that God has exempted us from long-term commitments. I believe that we need to be involved in the Great Commission in multiple ways. The world needs the good news we carry.

How about engaging in dialogue with those who have been successful in short-term and long-term missions? How about learning about home missions and urban ministries from fellowships that have been successful in these? Any energy spent on these can make us a stronger community of mission.

God wants His church to be a healthy one. In this article we have examined five ways Christian churches of all denominations can be healthier. How healthy is your church?

3

IF MY PEOPLE, WHO ARE CALLED
BY MY NAME, SHALL UNITE . . .

What was Jesus' greatest wish? I would say that His greatest wish was for the unity of all His disciples from all over the world. He prayed, "that all of them may be one" (John 17:20 NIV). There is no disunity between the Father and the Son. There is great unity and harmony within the Trinity. Jesus prayed that such great unity would also be found among us.

History

The history of the Christian church is one of divisions and discord. One may justify most of the historical divisions by saying that they were based on very strong and fundamentally different convictions. Conviction-based disagreements can be seen even in the New Testament. Divisions based on personalities (e.g., Paul and Apollos in 1 Corinthians 1:12) and those based on false teachings are addressed in the New Testament. Later in history, events such as the great Protestant Reformation caused much disunity within the body of Christ. Some may say that only one part of that division was the true body of Christ. In any case, while there have been many divisions, there have also been many efforts to bring about Christian unity. The modern ecumenical movement and the Catholic–Pentecostal dialogue are examples of such efforts.

This article is not about such global unity of the body of Christ. I am now more concerned about the disunity among us—Pentecostal/charismatic people in America, people of like precious faith. I believe that it is in our power and interest to change the current situation.

Denominations

I am not an anti-denominational fellow. Denominations have a positive role to play in most societies. But an excessive level of denominational spirit can cause loss and damage to the Lord's work. Denominations of similar faith, on the other hand, if they act in a spirit of unity, can accomplish much for the Lord.

I once wrote an article calling all the Pentecostal groups in America to come under one umbrella of some kind for the sake of our effectiveness as a Pentecostal community in a postmodern situation. I suggested this only because I am convinced that together we have the potential to do much greater works than the ones we are now undertaking separately.

I can see some people laughing at this proposal. That's okay. I would rather be known as a person who could love all God's people, especially those in the Spirit-filled tradition. I want to be known as a person who could see God's purposes beyond personal preferences and ego needs. I don't care if a person outside my fellowship became a prominent leader. I want to be remembered as a minister who believed that Jesus' prayer for unity was a goal worth pursuing, even if that meant personal loss of power or opportunities.

Pilgrims and Aliens

Please don't misunderstand. I do not feel that all the Pentecostal denominations all over the world have to unite to become one body—although they also need to work in unity—because they do not live in the spiritually threatening position we in America find ourselves in. We are truly pilgrims and aliens here. We can spread the gospel faster only if we can speak with one common voice. If that is not possible, then we, as members of various churches and denominations, should at least pledge to work together in unity for the sake of the kingdom of God.

I am thankful to see the efforts being made in various circles in this spirit of unity. We should wholeheartedly support these efforts. The kingdom of God is not meat, drink, or ego (see Rom. 4:17). It is righteousness, peace, and joy in the Holy Spirit. God is moving by His Spirit all over the world. He has placed us in America for such a time as this for some divine purposes. If we can work in unity, God's purposes will be accomplished in us and through us.

Benefits

There are several things we can do together in unity. We can find occasions to worship together. We can hold united conventions and conferences to help ourselves spiritually and to propagate the gospel. We can engage in evangelistic and missionary work locally and globally. We can raise significant monies to promote God's work in other nations. We can conduct seminars and workshops for children, youth, and adults. We can have better training and continuing education programs for our ministers. We can find solutions to common problems. We can raise significant funds for various charitable ministries. We may even be able to establish schools and training centers to address the unique needs of the twenty-first century.

The world knows that we are Christians by our love. Our unity is the most visible evidence of our love for God and for one another. It is time to overcome racism and other historical problems that have caused disunity among Christians. We should not allow minor differences and personal ambitions to keep us from working in unity. Instead of using our energies to reinforce the walls that separate us, let us extend our hearts and hands to each other in love and unity.

4

THE PATMOS PERSPECTIVE: DEFINING REVIVAL

According to several reports, the Hindus of India and Muslims of the Middle East are now experiencing religious revivals. Revivals in these religions are marked by the increased participation of their adherents in religious rituals, intolerance of other religions, and the expanded political influence of their leaders. As Christians in general, and those in America in particular, are longing for a revival, it is appropriate to ask, "What is true Christian revival? And what does a Christian revival look like?"

Merriam-Webster defines *revival* as a period of renewed religious interest or an often highly emotional evangelistic meeting or series of meetings.[2] Unfortunately, even some Christians seem to think this is an adequate definition. But is this all there is to a Christian revival?

---

2 *Merriam-Webster Dictionary*, s.v. "revival," accessed February 2018, https://www.merriam-webster.com/dictionary/revival.

From a biblical perspective, revival can be defined in several ways. Assuming that John the apostle, exiled on the Island of Patmos near the end of the first century AD, was experiencing a revival, the following is an attempt to define revival from what might be called a "Patmos perspective."

1. Revival is hearing the voice of God in a noisy world.

John found himself on a "noisy" island. One can only imagine his conditions: the roar of wild animals, the cries of the fowls of the air, and the crashing waves of the Aegean Sea added to his noisy conditions. But in this situation, John heard the voice of the Lord Jesus (Rev. 1:10).

The people of God hearing the voice of God is a unique characteristic of Christian revival. One can hear God's voice only with reverence and humility. The voice of God is heard in prayer. It is also heard in the preaching of His Word; and the Word of God becomes the voice of God in revival preaching.

Hearing the voice of God follows an encounter with God. Abraham heard the voice of God when Lot was unable to hear it (Genesis 18). Moses heard the voice of God when Aaron was preoccupied with the golden calf (Deut. 9:15–16). Samuel heard the voice of God while Eli and his sons could not (1 Samuel 3). Elijah heard the voice of God when Ahab could not hear it (1 Kings 17:2). Isaiah heard the voice of God after an encounter with the Holy One (Isa. 6:8). Paul heard the voice of God when his fellow passengers on a sinking ship were hearing only their own fearful hearts (Acts 27:23–24). Today we live in a very noisy world. Sounding cymbals are everywhere. Politics and religion have become too loud. We, too, need to hear the voice of God.

2. Revival is experiencing the power of God in a powerless world.

Again, we examine John's experience on Patmos. From everything we know about his situation, he was in a very weak position: He was aged and alone. His coworkers had all been separated from him. Many had died. His own citizenship was in trouble. But John testifies that he was in the Spirit on the Lord's Day (Rev. 1:10). What an experience!

John experienced the power of God in a powerless condition. This is another characteristic of a true revival. The power of God manifests in Christian revivals and transforms human lives. John was transformed by this power, and it enlarged his vision.

The manifestation of God's power is not limited to what is normally considered "signs and wonders." His power manifests itself also in transformed lives and enlarged visions. Human might, manipulation, intimidation, or ego display cannot substitute for the genuine revelation of God's power. Just as one cannot carry fire in his pocket without getting burned, so also one cannot play with the power of God without consequences, for, as Hebrews 12:29 tells us, God is a consuming fire.

Our world is in desperate need of God's power. The popularity of the New Age religion and the occult is evidence of this hunger. Catering to the curiosity of today's multimedia generation, with its overstimulated senses, is not the purpose of the manifestation of the Holy Spirit. The Egyptian magicians created snakes from rods, just as Moses did, but Aaron's staff swallowed up the Egyptian staffs (Exod. 7:12). God's power does more than match the magician's tricks—God's power confirms His Word. It breaks the yoke of abuse and addictions.

In true revival, the revived themselves ultimately become signs and wonders!

3. Revival is seeing the glory of God in a dark world.

Patmos was a spiritually dark place. John was not sent there by the authorities to receive some kind of illumination. However, illumination is what he received. John reports how he turned and saw the face of Jesus, and he describes that glorious vision with vivid details (Rev. 1:12–16).

Only those who once had life can have a revival. John had seen the face of Jesus before. He had seen the glory of Jesus on the Mount of Transfiguration (Matt. 17:1–2). "We beheld his glory," he said of that experience, "the glory of the only begotten" (John 1:14 KJV). But that was long ago and far away from Patmos. Now years had gone by. Colleagues who'd shared that experience with him also had gone. Facing the end of his century, John needed a revival—a new revelation—and he received it as he saw the glory of God in the face of Jesus Christ.

It is interesting to note that as a young man, John had stood alone at the foot of the cross of Calvary, where Jesus suffered and died. As an old man, he was visited by Jesus on Patmos, where John had been banished—and the beloved disciple was refreshed by this visit. This was John's revival time.

Glittering cities and shining skyscrapers hide the darkness of our world today. But how we need the light of His face! The glory of God is found in the face of Jesus Christ. We must seek His face. There is no revival without Jesus, no light outside His light. We must desire His light. True revival is the spiritual experience of "seeing" the face of Jesus.

Isaiah saw the glory of God and cried out, "Woe is me!" (Isaiah 6:5 KJV). John fell at the feet of Jesus on Patmos (Rev. 1:17). Christian revival does not lift up the self. Instead, it calls the self to willing surrender to the lordship of Jesus Christ, and a life surrendered to Christ reflects the light of His glory into our dark world.

5

THE REVIVAL I DESIRE

Reports of revival are coming from all the continents of the earth. As the world inches its way toward the halfway point of a new century, in a new millennium, it seems that God is moving by His Spirit in a new way all over the world. History tells us that the beginning of the twentieth century also witnessed a worldwide spiritual awakening. Today's Pentecostal/Charismatic movement is the outgrowth of that revival.

The world has seen many revivals. The day of Pentecost was the beginning of the greatest one in history. Peter and the other apostles of the Lord Jesus were the human instruments of that divine intervention. Many centuries later, the Reformation became a mighty revival. People such as Luther, Calvin, and Zwingli became its human leaders. The Holiness revival that inspired the founding of the Methodist movement was another historic revival. God used John Wesley and others mightily in that revival. We are familiar with the Colonial revival in America and the names behind it, such as Edwards and Finney.

Others, such as the Welsh revival involving Evan Roberts, and the Pentecostal revival with Charles Parham, are also familiar to us. During the 1950s and '60s, people such as Oral Roberts, T. L. Osborn, Kathryn Kuhlman, and others, led the Charismatic revival, which emphasized healing. Many of today's revivalists are disciples of these leaders.

It is difficult to name the true leaders of today's revival. Only time will tell who will emerge as the leading personalities in the long run. Many Westerners perceive places such as Toronto and Pensacola as modern centers of revival, although there is no unanimous agreement on this among Pentecostals.

I am sharing a brief history of revivals to encourage my Pentecostal friends to expect another outpouring of this nature. The truth is that we all need another revival. Let me explain to you what type of revival I desire.

I want a revival that contains the best of all the revivals we have had throughout history. I am saying this with the awareness that each revival had a specific emphasis, and acknowledging that to order an all-inclusive revival may not be realistic. Nonetheless, as a third-generation Pentecostal, I long for a true revival that embodies the best of all God has. To ascertain the best qualities of the revivals we have seen and heard about, we can take a brief look at the ones I mentioned earlier.

The first and foremost quality evident in these revivals is an emphasis and reliance on the Word of God for authority and guidance. Although people questioned the initial manifestations of these revivals, the revivalists were eventually able to demonstrate the authenticity of what was happening based on the Bible. They never felt that anything else, including personal revelations, weighed above the written Word of God. This was especially true of the modern Pentecostal revival. Although people attacked early Pentecostals concerning speaking in tongues, the leaders were able to show its authenticity from the Word of God. Dependence on God's Word helped to establish truth and identify false doctrines.

Secondly, there was a concern and caution about what the Pentecostals called the "wildfire." Godly men and women watched over the people of God to protect them from the enemy's attacks and counterfeits.

Third, there was an emphasis on prayer and brotherly love. We must keep in mind that during the period of segregation in America, the early Pentecostals practiced racial harmony through the Holy Spirit.

Fourth, the earlier revivals propelled missionary concerns. People who were touched by the revivals were concerned about the salvation of peoples and nations, and they were willing to go into every person's world with the power of the gospel. They wanted signs and wonders to promote the kingdom of God on the earth.

Finally, personal integrity was valued by all previous revivals. People who failed in this area ultimately failed in ministry. We live at a time when people seem to be separating performance from character. This may be popular in certain secular areas, but for the disciples of Jesus, integrity is a requirement. The fruit of the Spirit must be evident in the lives of ministers and lay people. Lies about oneself or one's ministry were not tolerated in the long run. Truth was allowed to prevail, and the consequences followed.

The revival I desire has the following qualities: I want the Word of God to have the last say on all issues. I want the true fire of God and not anything else, regardless of how attractive or powerful it might be. I want a revival that emphasizes prayer and brotherly love. I want a revival that promotes evangelism and missions, with emphasis on signs, wonders, miracles, and healings. I want to see the manifestation of all the gifts of the Spirit. I want a revival that values the fruits of the Spirit, and expects integrity and holy living from all spiritual leaders. In summary, I want a revival that has the best of all the revivals we have experienced and heard about. "[O Lord!] Will you not revive us again, that your people may rejoice in you?" (Ps. 85:6 NIV).

6

THE FUTURE OF PENTECOSTALISM: REFORMATION OR RETREAT?

The Catholic Church of the sixteenth century was in need of reformation. Church leadership was hungry for power and willing to claim and keep it at any cost. They were not satisfied with just ecclesiastical power; they wanted real political power as well. The cry of the humble fell on deaf ears in those days. Theology was subject to change based on revenue needs. The church had become a mega organization with incredible powers—far from the *ekklesia* of the New Testament.

The sixteenth-century church was truly backslidden, but the hierarchy was in no mood to admit any need for a reformation. At such a time, God raised up people with strong vision and commitment to call for drastic change. Luther, Zwingli and others were among these passionate reformers. Interestingly, the ones God used to lead the Reformation were academics who were also competent clergy. Similarly, the modern Pentecostal movement was led by clergy educators.

Today's Pentecostal churches are not in a backslidden condition, like the sixteenth-century church, but Pentecostals are guilty of losing their spiritual momentum and values. They are guilty of creating unnecessary hierarchies and unaccountable independents. They are guilty of engaging in power struggles, political wars, and worldly elections. They are guilty of not separating Pentecostal traditions from vital Pentecostal teachings and of defending all of them with equal passion at the expense of vitality and growth. They are guilty of only thinking locally in a global world, especially in terms of nonessential denominational rules versus the mandate to evangelize.

Sociologists tell us that movements become organizations in time. They lose the initial energy and vitality in this process. Organizations are self-preserving by nature. In the effort to preserve themselves as organizations, the original divine movements die and status quo prevails.

Pentecostals have come a long way from their humble beginnings. They now boast social acceptance and organizational assets. Headquarters buildings, Bible colleges and seminaries, bylaws and pay scales are indications that the organizations are doing well, but they are no guarantee that the movement—the organism—is still flourishing and impacting the world in powerful ways.

We should not start in the Spirit and end in the flesh. So also we should not start as a dynamic movement and end as lifeless organizations. That is why I believe we need a Pentecostal Reformation. We cannot blame denominational leaders for the lack of positive changes within the churches. Leaders are elected basically to preserve and grow the organizations. They cannot make decisions that rock the organizations. So by the very nature of their positions, they are not able to take big steps, even if they want to. They also can get replaced if they go too fast. Changing an organization is like turning a big ship: it takes much time and effort.

The Christian church is capable of reforming itself. Christian theology allows it. Renewal and reformation have been part of our history. Not all religions are capable of doing this. For instance, there are scholars who believe that behind the violent segment of Islam is a cry for reformation; but Islam may not be capable of reforming itself due to the nature of its theology. Where there is no reformation, suicide bombers are born!

The modern Pentecostal movement is the child of reformations. Pentecostal roots include Catholicism, Orthodoxy, Protestantism, Evangelicalism, and the Holiness movement. Pentecostalism is the result of reformations in these branches of the Christian church. But Pentecostals are in need of a reformation today. Those who believe this should not remain silent any longer.

We need to seriously consider if the global growth of the Charismatic movement is an indication that Pentecostals need a reformation. We need an honest dialogue about this topic. False doctrines in some streams of the Charismatic movement should not stop us from engaging in such a conversation non-defensively. Such a discussion may show us a path to reformation, and it requires academics—theological educators who respect the church and who are concerned for its future—and church leaders who love God's work more than they love their own personal positions or gains.

We have to acknowledge that renewal often comes from the margins. God is at work in the margins of society. In fact, Pentecostalism came from the margins. Now we are so center-oriented. Today's God-ordained reformers may not be at the center of the circle or the top of the organizational chart. It was so even in the book of Acts. The fire of God was burning in Samaria and Antioch, far from Jerusalem, where the leaders were. But the leaders of that day had the wisdom to send delegates to the margin to see what God was doing there. They also had the spiritual sensitivity to not quench that fire. We need such leaders still.

Reforming will begin only with a true self-examination in the form of honest dialogue. It will take members of the Pentecostal academy as well as ecclesiastical leaders. God decides the time of revivals. But I am of the opinion that reformers will have a chance to take the first steps toward the next Pentecostal revival.

7

LOCAL CHURCH AND
CHRISTIAN EDUCATION

Although Christian conversion is an internal matter, the Christian life displays external evidence. The New Testament documents biographies of individuals whose lives were transformed by an encounter with Jesus. The Samaritan woman who met Jesus at the well was changed by that encounter (John 4:39), and the demoniac who met Jesus received a sound mind (Luke 8:35). Similarly, the despised tax collector Zacchaeus became a philanthropist as he met Jesus in Jericho (Luke 19:8).

The story of the Ethiopian eunuch testifies that an encounter with Jesus through the mediation of an evangelist is as powerful as an encounter with Jesus in the flesh. Philip introduced the Ethiopian to Jesus on a desert road in Gaza. The eunuch accepted Christ, was baptized in water in the desert, and went home rejoicing (Acts 8:38)! In the same manner, the jailer who imprisoned Paul and Silas accepted Christ and was instantly transformed. His sins were washed away and he washed the apostle's wounds

(Acts 16:33–34). The largest portion of the New Testament was written by Paul the persecutor, who met Jesus and became the persecuted.

The change that Jesus facilitates in the lives of believers normally manifests in the decisions they make. This is where Christian education becomes significant. Christian education must equip believers to make choices that will glorify God. A Christian must exhibit a lifestyle that is different from that of a non-Christian. Ultimately, an individual's lifestyle is the outcome of the decisions and choices that person makes.

The Bible gives examples of good and bad decisions and choices. For example, Cain made the bad decision to murder his brother (Gen. 4:8). Esau decided to sell his birthright (Gen. 25:29–34), and Samson chose to confess the secret of his strength to Delilah (Judg. 16:15–17). King Saul decided to disobey God and keep the enemy alive (1 Sam. 15:20). The rich young ruler decided to walk away from the invitation given by Jesus (Matt. 19:16–22). Demas decided to forsake Paul because he loved the world (2 Tim. 4:10), and Governor Felix chose not to make a decision for Christ (Acts 24:24–26).

Thankfully, the Bible presents clear instructions about the healthy choices we must make. We are to choose unity rather than division (Phil. 2:2; 1 Peter 3:3). Forgiveness is a better choice than bitterness (Matt. 6:14–15; Mark 11:25; Heb. 12:15; James 5:16), and we must choose holiness rather than worldliness (Rom. 12:2; 1 John 2:15). Love is a better choice than hatred (1 John 3:15; 4:7–8), and healing is a better choice than brokenness (John 5:6–9).

Psychologists were not the first ones to say that happiness is a choice; the Bible also teaches this principle. The apostle

Paul pleaded with the Philippian believers to choose happiness, saying, "Rejoice in the Lord always. I will say it again: Rejoice" (Phil. 4:4 NIV). In the Old Testament, Joshua made the most important decision: "As for me and my house, we will serve the LORD" (Josh. 24:15 KJV).

Many churchgoers are simply cultural Christians. They remind me of many Indian Hindus, who are cultural Hindus and nothing more. It is the duty of Christian educators to raise the level of biblical literacy and Christian discipleship in our churches. Bible college and seminary professors have noticed an astounding level of biblical illiteracy in incoming students. This appears to be a great problem. The remedy can only spring out of the local church, which must raise up disciples of Jesus who know the Word of God to the degree that they are able to evaluate their culture and make truly Christian decisions on a daily basis. Sometimes the word *decision* in the Pentecostal vocabulary is limited to the decision to accept Christ, but we must train people for lifelong decisions. The church must equip believers to make morally right decisions. Only competent, Spirit-filled Christian education can accomplish this awesome task.

I must say a word concerning our attitude about adult Christian education. Unfortunately, Pentecostals still conduct the ministry of education as if only children and young people need educating. I don't know how we can maintain this attitude in today's world. There was a time when education was over at an early age, but the world in which that took place no longer exists. We live in a different world, in a different age—a fast-changing, knowledge-hungry information age. Education is no longer limited to younger people. Adult education is a very fast-growing field because people in all fields are constantly studying to update their knowledge. People of all ages in science, technology, and other fields are not ashamed to continue their education. They know that their existence and success depend on it. Even megachurch pastors are going back to school to update their knowledge and skills. Why is the church ashamed of adult Christian education? Is it because of the false pride of its members?

Adult Christians need to attend Sunday school classes or Bible classes. Of course, adults and children do not have the same learning needs. Each group needs an appropriate curriculum. There are experts in Bible, theology, and pedagogy who can develop such curriculums for churches and Bible Schools. Our churches must consider this matter seriously. It is high time for us to move Christian education to include students of all ages.

8

CHURCH GROWTH
AND PASTORAL CARE

I am a third-generation Pentecostal minister who lives in a city with fast-growing Pentecostal/charismatic churches. I rejoice in the growth of our movement and believe the Lord wants our churches to grow. My concern is this: How can pastors cope with the increasing demands of their growing congregations without becoming burned-out?

Before my move to Oral Roberts University, I was privileged to pastor one of the fastest-growing Pentecostal churches in southern New England. As that church grew to become one of the largest Protestant congregations in the city, I encountered many practical problems, particularly in the area of pastoral care.

Since I have had clinical training and experience in pastoral care and counseling, I have encountered individuals and families from all denominations, often meeting them during crises. I have become increasingly concerned about the lack of attention given to the area of pastoral care in our growing churches, in both Pentecostal and charismatic congregations.

In our complex society, the need for pastoral care is great. Many pastors have begun to acknowledge this need and are seeking creative ways to meet the challenge. They have learned that ignoring the problem will not solve it.

The biblical model of a pastor is that of a shepherd. The Old Testament proposed this model, and our Lord endorsed it. The relationship between the shepherd and the sheep is a sacred one, for which there is no substitute.

Church growth can force pastors to spend all of their working hours as preachers and administrators. This model of ministry may allow pastors to feed their sheep, but does not guarantee proper caregiving. A pastor who is not available for caregiving in effect becomes an evangelist whose ministry focuses on short-term goals. A pastor/teacher should be more than a preacher/teacher. A pastor/teacher must be more than an information distributor. Church members should be able to get to know their pastors better than they know their local newscasters.

Growing churches must consider adding specially trained pastoral care ministers to assist the senior pastor. Leadership in pastoral care should be provided by people who have both training and experience; it should not be left to the uninitiated. However, it must be remembered that specialists cannot replace the pastor; they can only extend a shepherd's ministry. This is a painful truth.

Our Bible colleges also must give greater emphasis to pastoral care and Bible-based counseling. Today's pastors must be able to do more than quote Scripture verses to people in crisis; they must be competent to counsel. Local churches need to utilize outside pastoral care personnel, such as chaplains, to train lay caregivers. One-shot training is not sufficient; people must receive ongoing training in caregiving and altar ministry.

Church growth sustained by competent caregiving will bear more fruit. A current example of efforts to meet this need is the Stephen Ministries program for church laypersons, which trains the layperson to provide skilled listening to members and to recognize when a referral to professional counseling is the right choice. I am familiar with several churches that have begun such a program.

Another effort to provide pastoral caregiving within a large church setting is the cell-group method. Victory Christian Center in Tulsa, Oklahoma, is one church that provides annual conferences as well as regular classes specifically designed to impart to cell-group leaders the skills needed for wise leadership. Victory's small fellowship groups are an integral component of the larger church's function. David (Paul) Yonggi Cho has written books describing this method's successful use in maintaining effective pastoral caregiving within the church he pioneered in South Korea.

This is not written with the intention of increasing the pastor's burden; neither is it an argument against church growth or lay ministry. It presents the hope that a more effective, more fruitful church growth can be sustained. It envisions a vital church with a powerful sense of community, *koinonia*, and caring—a truly biblical church.

9

DOING CHURCH
AT THE BORDER OF
BUSINESS AND BUSINESSLIKE

The language of business is replacing biblical and theological vocabulary in many churches and ministries across the world. Terms such as *market share, marketing, public relations, needs analysis, customer satisfaction, environmental scanning, strategic plan, change management, efficiency*, and so forth, are replacing *evangelism, discipleship, compassion, Christian education, faith promise, caring*, and the like, in many places. A similar change in church vocabulary took place a generation ago when psychology made its way into the churches and provided an additional model of pastoral ministry and a new image of pastor as therapist.

Business concepts are important and can certainly contribute to the efficient operation of the organizational aspects of the community of faith. The problem is that the border between business and businesslike is disappearing at a fast pace. No, some unscrupulous people are not responsible for this. It is actually the result of good people with very good intentions applying excellent business concepts to the body of Christ without adequate biblical and theological reflection. They are simply adapting good business principles and practices without "baptizing" them.

Here's the problem: The church is not simply an organization; it is primarily a living organism. The Bible does not dwell on the organizational aspects of the church; instead, it uses familial language to describe the church. The church is the family of God, the community of faith, the body of Christ, and the household of faith. A family is not about bottom line. It is about relationships and stewardship. It is a place of sacrifices and nurturing, not profit, profit-sharing, customer satisfaction, and normal concepts of return on investment.

No doubt, the church has always been involved with the marketplace. Marketplace must be a context of ministry and a contributor to missions. However, the church is not simply a business. The difference between business and businesslike must be preserved in the context of the church and its ministries.

Three business concepts have contributed to the confusion in this regard—leadership, change, and efficiency. There are three troublesome assumptions behind these concepts: everyone must be a leader, all changes are good and needed, and efficiency is the highest value in all situations. Let's briefly examine these.

Leadership. The Bible says very little about leadership as this concept is understood in today's society. Scripture talks much more about *followership*! *Leader* is not a frequent word in the Bible. We are advised to remember our leaders and to imitate their faith, but we are called to take up the cross and follow Jesus. God calls certain people to lead others, but the spirit in which they lead is not arrogance; it is service. In the kingdom of God, leaders are not CEOs; they are servants and followers at the same time. Biblical leaders are to invite others to follow them only as they follow Christ. Not everyone should be a leader in the body of Christ. It is okay to be a follower in the family of God.

Change. Although institutions must be flexible enough to adapt to changes around them, the idea that constant change is what is needed in all situations is not true. Some changes are unnecessary and damaging. Some things should be left alone. There is no need to repair unbroken things.

Efficiency. Efficiency is a good thing, but there are higher values than efficiency in some situations. A grandmother may not be the most efficient member of the family, but do you want to replace her? Tithing may not be the most efficient financial management by some measures, but do you want to stop giving to God? Raising children is not the most efficient way to spend money, but do you want to disown your children? No, certainly not. Efficiency is important, but sometimes there are other values that are more important. Relationships matter. Compassion matters. Here's the truth: sometimes ministry is inefficient.

So here I stand. The church is not a business, but its organizational aspects must be operated like a business. Many churches and ministries are guilty of sloppy and sometimes illegal operations and business practices. Applying excellent business practices to the organizational dimension of the church is good Christian stewardship, but great caution must be taken not to blur the lines between the life and mission of the body of Christ and its operational responsibilities. The church of Jesus Christ in the world today is both an organism and an organization at the same time. The organization must serve the organism. It should never be the other way.

10

WHAT PENTECOSTALS AND CHARISMATICS CAN LEARN FROM EACH OTHER

I am a third-generation Pentecostal minister. My grandfather was a pioneer preacher of the Pentecostal message in Kerala, India. My father led thirty Pentecostal churches in the Mavelikara district of Kerala. Following their footsteps and giving up the dream to be a physicist, I prepared to become a Pentecostal minister in a very non-Pentecostal place—Yale University Divinity School—and was ordained in a classical Pentecostal denomination in the United States. After pastoring a church in New England for five years, I wound up joining a charismatic organization—the Oral Roberts Ministries and the related Oral Roberts University in Tulsa, Oklahoma.

I started my work at Oral Roberts University as a chaplain, then became a professor in the seminary, and later was appointed dean of the College of Theology and Ministry. These positions allowed me close proximity to a number of movers and shakers of the Charismatic movement as well as several notable leaders of the Pentecostal churches.

As a city at the center of the United States, where the world headquarters of the ministries of globally influential charismatic leaders such as T. L. Osborn, Oral Roberts, and Kenneth Hagin Sr. are located, Tulsa is rightfully known as the charismatic capital of the world. Many well-known ministries around the world trace their roots to Tulsa. My position at Oral Roberts University made it possible for me to see the great leaders of the Charismatic movement in action. As all sorts of teachings came though Tulsa, I became an eyewitness to genuine manifestations of the Spirit as well as the most incredible ego trips and excesses.

Through my preaching ministry among the native and immigrant Pentecostals in America, I also witnessed genuine moves of God along with undeniable legalism and hypocrisy. While Pentecostals listed the theological weaknesses of the Charismatic movement, they kept reporting decreasing memberships, a drastically reduced number of Spirit-filled people in their churches (especially young people), and an increasing number of ineffective ministers (these facts can be documented). While bragging on the correctness of their doctrines, Pentecostals seemed busy building their denominational institutions. Institutionalization of a powerful movement seemed to make it ineffective during this period.

I believe Pentecostals and charismatics can learn from each other and benefit the kingdom of God. What could they learn from each other? Let me just mention one item for each group. First, the Pentecostals can learn fresh lessons of faith, healing, and giving that the charismatics are teaching. Likewise, the charismatics can learn the importance of major biblical doctrines and a balanced ministry from the Pentecostals. As a result, the Pentecostals may be surprised to find out that they are simply going back to their own roots. And the charismatics might find out that only sound doctrines will prevail in the long run.

11

EVANGELISM IN THE NEW AGE

Whether we live in India or America, we do not live in the same world into which we were born. In a sense, we are all immigrants, and like all immigrants, we struggle to adjust to our new world. Born in the age of bullock carts and steam engine trains, as some of us were, we now live in the age of supersonic jets and space vehicles. I remember when we had to bicycle our way to distant places in India to share some important news. Today we have wireless phones and satellite communication facilities everywhere. We no longer depend on the old bikes for fast communication.

I recall how just a couple of decades ago, a cable sent from the United States took three days to get to India. I don't send cables anymore; instead, I dial direct and the phone rings in a remote place in Asia within moments.

What are the powers that are changing our world? I believe that there are seven forces at work that shape the modern world. Ignoring these can seriously hinder our evangelistic efforts.

Seven Forces That Shape the Modern World

1. Science and Technology

The strongest force impacting our world is technology. It has moved us from old typewriters to new computers. Television, cell phones, computers, the internet, and so many other inventions have changed our lives. *National Geographic* conducted a report some time ago on the glowing television sets in the tents of homeless people in Calcutta. Many of them operate on stolen electricity. Technology is enslaving modern man. When we were young, children played ball outdoors, but now many sit idly on couches and play video games all day.

2. Knowledge

Information is the second force shaping today's world. The internet has created an information superhighway. Knowledge is flowing in full color on the internet. One can log on from anywhere and study any subject at any time. We have increasing knowledge, but we lack wisdom. We have information, but we do not know how to evaluate the information. We do not know what is trustworthy and what is not. We have a second generation now that receives information without supervision.

3. Cultural Change and Speed of Life

The globe is becoming a cultural melting pot. Our world is changing so fast that people feel as if they are passengers on a roller coaster. Easy access to multimedia and increasing opportunities for world travel are causing people to adopt foreign cultures into their own. Old men in India are clad in suits, while mainstream women in America wear nose rings! Cultural barriers are being removed. Unfortunately, some have adopted all new things while others are resisting change completely. This has produced cultural clashes all over the world. Violence has become common, "ethnic cleansing" has entered our vocabulary, and time has become a rare commodity. We have instant weddings! Instant meetings! Instant Coffee! Ta-ta! Bye-bye!

4. New Spirituality

Fed up with materialism, the world has adopted a new spirituality. This spirituality is one without God. Modern man believes, not in God, but in a Force! Generally speaking, there is no acknowledgment of God the Father, God the Son, or God the Holy Spirit. The New Age religion is a mix of Hinduism, Buddhism, and Christianity. Ayurveda is sold as spirituality in America, and extreme environmentalism is a religion for many. Today's pseudo-spirituality has no ten commandments to guide it. It affirms all alternate lifestyles, and tolerance is its highest virtue.

5. Broken Families

There was a time when Indian immigrants could brag about their strong families. Even non-Christian immigrants had strong family ties. This is not the case anymore. Many immigrant families are falling apart. Working parents have no time for their children. Earphones blast modern music into our youth's brains so they do not hear their parents, even when they are around. Divorce is a major problem. This is not surprising since we get more training to ride a bike than to remain married.

6. Money Is God

The love of money has always existed, but this generation has taken that concept to new heights. Man is willing to do anything for a few dollars. "Keeping up with the Joneses" requires a lot of borrowing, and many cannot afford to pay back the debts. Some parents have no values to give their children, only stocks!

7. Hopelessness

Ours is a hopeless age. There is no real cure for AIDS or Alzheimer's. Heart disease and cancer are still medical challenges. The rich get richer and the poor become poorer. Newspapers are filled with news of killings and suicides, and illicit drugs are everywhere. There is a pill for every ailment. The inventors of Prozac, the antidepressant, are becoming billionaires!

Twenty-First-Century Evangelism

How shall we evangelize the inhabitants of such an age? I believe that our evangelistic efforts must take into account all these forces that are shaping our world. Let me propose some ideas to be included in a strategic plan to evangelize the twenty-first century.

1. Use technology to spread the gospel. Since television and the internet are today's marketplaces, we can bring the message of the gospel to these places in the same way that we brought it to the marketplaces through open-air meetings. We must not compromise the gospel, but we should be willing to change our evangelistic methods.

2. Train ministers at a higher level. The knowledge level of the population is increasing; consequently, ministers must be given better education for ministry. Bible schools must move

beyond being cottage industries. We need Bible schools and seminaries that can combine academics with spiritual empowerment and practical skills. Pastors need to learn leadership skills and conflict resolution. We need to end the tendency of Bible schools to produce only Bible school teachers. Our Bible schools must move to a higher level to produce practicing pastors and evangelists. Ultimately, we need Bible schools and seminaries that produce apostles, prophets, evangelists, pastors, and teachers.

3. We must offer spiritually refreshing ministries to people living in today's fast-paced society. We should be attracting unbelievers with a gospel that heals. To make this possible, we must come up with creative ways to attract nonbelievers to the good news.

4. We must preach and teach biblical spirituality, not just cultural Christianity or insensitive versions of Pentecostalism. Instead of preaching about food and clothes, we must preach Jesus Christ and Him crucified. Emphasize life transformation rather than religious dress code!

5. Attract souls through programs that strengthen marriage and family life. People must be taught how to be good husbands, wives, and parents. Counseling seminars, camp meetings, marriage classes, parenting seminars, and so on, are means to attract people to the Lord Jesus. These programs will also benefit believers.

6. Practice lifestyle evangelism. Our lifestyle must reflect our faith so that our preaching and practice match. We must live as if Christ—not material things—is our treasure. This requires that we learn to share our material goods with others in need. Believers must be taught to give tithes and offerings. Giv-

ing is not just for Americans; all God's people must be givers. For this to happen, pastors must teach the blessings of giving in the name of Jesus. We must have ways and means to assist unbelievers in need.

7. Be people of hope. It is crucial that unbelievers see our hope in Christ; thus we must adopt a lifestyle based on hope. If we let others see how we handle disappointments, they will see our hope in the midst of crises. People who watch our lives must see Christ in us, the hope of glory!

12

PASTORS WHO RELATE TO PEOPLE AS EVANGELISTS

The apostle Paul tells us in Ephesians 4:11–13 that pastors and evangelists are gifts of God to the church. Both offices and functions are needed to build up the body of Christ. However, pastors and evangelists do not relate to people quite the same way. It pays to know the basic mode by which you relate to people. As a pastor, how do you relate to those under your ministry? Do you relate pastorally? Or do you relate evangelistically?

Pastoral ministry is a relational ministry. Although pastors do evangelistic work—preaching and presenting the gospel message—the primary mode of their relationships with the flock must be shepherdlike. Pastoral care involves not only the message, but also an ongoing relationship with the messenger.

People know that the evangelist will move on, but they expect a long-term relationship with their pastor. Pastors who insist on relating to their people as evangelists, focusing only on the message and not on the ongoing relationship, deprive their people and themselves of the richness of the pastoral experience. Pastoral relationships have been ordained by the Lord.

Evangelism, on the other hand, is a propositional ministry. Its focus is on the message rather than the relationship. There is such a thing as relational evangelism, but by the very nature of their work, evangelists tend to concentrate on the evangel—the good news. They share the message and invite the listeners to respond to that message.

Evangelists must be careful not to get involved in pastoral relationships. This can give rise to difficult situations because they contribute to role conflicts. Good evangelists leave the ongoing relationships to the pastors. While it is easy for a pastor to misunderstand and criticize an evangelist's mode of relationship or envy the luxury of terminating relationships, it is also easy for an evangelist to be unaware of the depth of the pastor's commitment to ongoing care. Evangelists who insist that pastors must relate like themselves render them a disservice. The fact is that the church needs both pastoral and evangelistic relationships. The stimulus of the evangelistic challenge is a good thing; so is the security of the ongoing pastoral relationship.

It is a valuable insight to recognize your own relational tendencies. Determining which is your primary mode of ministry can save you—and your flock—much grief. Reflect on your style of relationship with the flock: Is it pastoral, a relational ministry? Or are you more comfortable with an evangelical presentation, a propositional style of relating? Is your present ministry a good fit with your relational style?

Both pastoral and evangelistic relationships are vital to a thriving church. Please don't overemphasize one to the exclusion of the other.

13

A CHANGING CULTURE AND THE UNCHANGING GOSPEL

We live in a fast-changing world where we have become global villagers. Although there are still boundaries demarking nations, the internet and the many satellites orbiting the earth have blurred the boundaries between all nations to a great extent. No one really knows how to live in this new world.

It is almost impossible today for totalitarian regimes to lie to their own people for any length of time. Governments are not the sole sources of information any longer. Ordinary citizens can receive independent information to confirm or invalidate governmental claims. Russia, China, and the Czech Republic are all witnesses of this phenomenon. Things that happen in faraway places are brought to the living rooms through computers and television sets.

The blurring of boundaries between nations has brought the various cultures of the world together for the first time in human history. People are familiar with foreign cultures, languages, foods, and so on through television programs and increasing international travels. What they see and hear affects all people.

There was a time when only the elite could afford international travel. That is not the case now. Ordinary people can afford to travel. Even with all the new airports, air carriers cannot keep up with the demand for travel. Seats on international flights are sold out months in advance. People who travel are influenced by the cultures they visit. Often they adopt the ways of other people and nations. Suit-clad old men in India, thirsty preachers in Asia demanding Coca-Cola, and Americans wearing nose rings are all examples of this cultural infiltration.

Just a couple of decades ago, Westerners used to ask, "What is curry?" Now the long lines outside the Indian restaurants in America are made up of mostly non-Indians. Americans used to make fun of people who ate yogurt. Now the same people are eating yogurt for breakfast, lunch, and dinner. Movie stars are doing commercials for yogurt! Those who do not know how to wear a real sari are making dresses that look like saris. These things demonstrate cross-cultural infiltration.

We cannot suggest that all cultural changes are good. However, resisting all change is not necessarily good either. Cultural resistance often becomes cultural wars. We have already witnessed that some of these wars can end up becoming ethnic cleansing.

What are we supposed to do with the unchanging gospel in such a time as this? How shall we handle the unchanging gospel in these changing times? Shall we change the gospel to fit the culture? Of course, not. However, there are some things we can do to preserve the gospel and facilitate evangelism. Let me suggest some ideas here.

1. Believe the gospel and live it out in daily life. Make faith a matter of lifestyle. Stop being like the people of the world. They will know we are Christians by our love. Stop imitating worldly politics in God's church. Stop the fights for power and control.

2. Give priority to the Word of God rather than to our traditions. Stop majoring on minors. Don't let any tradition, no matter how dear that may be to us, have priority over the Word of God.

3. Don't marry the gospel with any particular human culture. Let the Bible critique all human cultures. The Word of God can judge Eastern and Western cultures. When we marry a particular culture with the gospel, the gospel becomes a slave of that culture, destined to go up and down with the fortunes of that culture. This is how Christianity, which has its roots in the East, became a Western religion in Asia. For instance, Christianity was married to the British culture, but the British were not very Christian about their dealings with India, and that destroyed Christianity's appeal to patriotic Indians. We should not correct that problem by creating a new marriage between Eastern culture and Christianity. The living water must be given to Indians in the Indian cup, but one should not get mixed up between the water and the cup!

I believe that we should preach less on dress codes and more about Jesus. I believe that it is foolish to spend our valuable time preaching about culture and fashions instead of the gospel of the kingdom of God. The kingdom of God is not meat or drink. God has not called us to propagate any man-made culture—Eastern or Western; we are called to transform all cultures through the power of the Holy Spirit. We must let the gospel influence all cultures. Then only can God's kingdom come on earth fully as it is in heaven!

14

MIXING THE MINISTRIES OF PASTORS AND PEOPLE

The Gospel of John tells us that God gave us His Son (3:16). The apostle Paul wrote to the Ephesians that God gave to the church some apostles, prophets, evangelists, pastors, and teachers (4:11). If one reads these passages carefully, one has to accept that just as Jesus is God's gift to the world, pastors are God's gift to His Church. Quite often people do not know how to treat a pastor, especially one with whom they have differences of opinion. The answer is that they should be treated as God's gifts. This is not to suggest that pastors are faultless creatures. This is far from true. However, all must remember that when a gift is abused, it is not the gift that feels insulted; it is the giver of that gift who endures the insult. We must find godly ways of dealing with our differences.

There are some churches where pastors do not allow anyone else to minister. They act as if everything should be done by them, and by them alone. They have such a tremendous need to control people and events that they are driven to do everything themselves. People are there just to be "ministered to."

The Bible does not instruct pastors to do everything in the church. Pastors, according to the Word of God, are servant-leaders, not lords. They are to lead God's people in the work of the ministry.

Take a moment now to reread Ephesians 4. We are told that God gave some apostles, prophets, evangelists, pastors, and teachers (this phrase should be more correctly translated "pastor-teachers") for the perfecting of the saints for the work of the ministry (KJV). The people of God, "the saints," have their ministries in the church. Pastors and other "set-apart" officers of the church are there to perfect the saints so that they can excel in their ministries in the church.

The churches of India, for example, have a tendency to consider evangelists as second-class or lower-grade pastors. Ephesians 4 does not support this view. The different offices of apostle, prophet, evangelist, and pastor-teacher are all honored by God.

What are the ministries of the members? Romans 12 lists these: Some are to prophesy, some are to serve and give. Others may administer, or organize. The list is long; the saints have many ministries. They must be allowed and encouraged to minister in the church, under the servant leadership of godly pastors.

Some churches have a reverse problem, viewing pastors as mere ceremonial heads. The people do everything and control everything; the pastor is just a paid employee. This denial of the servant-leadership role disgraces the gospel's instructions to the churches.

The ministries of pastors and lay people must be mixed in balance to do God's work effectively. All parties must fulfill God's call on their lives. Everything must be done decently and in order, according to the Word of God, for the glory of God through Jesus Christ our Lord, to be revealed through His body, the church. Saints must be encouraged to minister within the church under the servant leadership of godly pastors. And all must minister in humility.

15

MODERN MISSIONARIES: FROM EVERYWHERE TO EVERYWHERE

When the word *missionary* is mentioned, Asians visualize a Western face. It is a good testimony to the faithful services of Western missionaries in Asia for a long time. We must thank God for the sacrifices of these missionaries; however, it is high time for all to recognize that mission work seen as the exclusive labor of Westerners is a myth today. The power and authority Western churches had on the missionary enterprise have been on the decline for a number of years now.

In 1900, 34.5 percent of the global population was Christian and 66 percent of Christians called Europe their home.[3] Due to the sacrificial work and faithful labor of Westerners, Christianity spread across the East and the South. By the year 2015, only 23 percent of the world's Christians were Europe-

---

3 George Weigel, "World Christianity by the Numbers," *First Things*, February 25, 2015, n.p., https://www.firstthings.com/web-exclusives/2015/02/world-christianity-by-the-numbers.

ans as Christianity is fast growing outside its traditional home bases. The most extraordinary Christian growth over the past century took place in Africa. African Christian population has grown from 8.7 million in 1900 to 542 million today.[4] Christian faith was once seen as a Western religion. That is not the case today, although there are still people who choose to think of Christianity as the white man's religion.

The rapid growth of Christianity in the southern hemisphere is attributed to the African growth, global urbanization, and the rise of Pentecostalism which now claims 645 million adherents worldwide.[5] One cannot ignore the fact that the explosive growth of Christianity took place only after the colonial days of the last century.

According to Pew Research Center, 29 percent of the population of South Korea today is Christian.[6] Although America is still the number one missionary-sending nation, when one considers the other sending nations together, the majority of missionaries are now non-Americans.[7] As the current trend continues, nearly half of the top missionary-sending nations now are in the Global South.

The well-known book *The Next Christendom*, written by Professor Philip Jenkins, stated the obvious: the color of Christianity has changed from white to brown and black. Once the capital of Christianity was Rome or Constantinople,

---

4 Weigel, n.p.
5 Weigel, n.p.
6 http://www.pewresearch.org/fact-tank/2014/08/12/6-facts-about-christianity-in-south-korea/.
7 http://www.christianitytoday.com/pastors/2013/july-online-only/worlds-top-missionary-sending-country-will-surprise-you.html.

but Christianity's center of gravity has now shifted from the Northern Hemisphere to the Southern Hemisphere.

This is not pleasant news to Western Christians. They are still learning to deal with this new reality. They still hold significant power; however, with the rising of developing nations, more power is likely to move south. An estimated count of Christians in China is 115 million, but some believe that the actual number is higher.[8] Christianity is still growing in the West, but at a slower rate than in the East and South.

The issue is not whether Westerners or Easterners are in charge of world missions. The time has come for missionaries to go *from* everywhere *to* everywhere. This trend has already begun. For instance, several large churches in England are pastored by immigrants from Africa. These are not churches by the immigrants and for the immigrants. They are open to all, and many attendees are locals.

This is high time for the immigrant churches in America to consider how long they will close their doors to the natives of their adopted country. This is a crucial question, especially if this is the final hour and God's ultimate purpose for the current worldwide immigration is the evangelization of the world.

God needs Western missionaries *and* Eastern missionaries. He is looking for people from the North and the South to carry the good news of Jesus Christ to the rest of the world. He needs speakers and workers, preachers and professionals. God's plans for the world will be fulfilled only when disciples of Jesus will go from everywhere to everywhere and bear

---

8 https://thediplomat.com/2017/09/chinas-thriving-underground-churches-in-danger/.

witness to Christ. Only that will guarantee that people from every nation, tribe, and language will sing His praises at the impending gathering of saints.

16

THE NEW (TESTAMENT) WORLD ORDER

The new world order! It was a believable idea. I remember seeing President Ronald Reagan standing by the Berlin Wall and challenging the "iron curtain" it represented. Now it lay crumbled. Communism had fallen! The forces of darkness and evil seemed exposed and dying. History was being made at fast-forward speed. The new world order seemed to be at hand.

Then came the headlines: A great number of Russians voting for a known expansionist. Ethnic cleansing in Bosnia. Tribal massacres in Rwanda. Disaster looming in North Korea. Somalia. Haiti. Iraq. Major crises were popping up everywhere. The new world order began to look very much like the old world order.

The truth dawned on me then. The idea of a new world order did not originate with modern politicians. It began with Jesus Christ! But He was not talking about a man-centered, man-initiated, godless, and violent world order.

The new world order—the New *Testament* world order—
that Jesus envisioned is called the kingdom of God. It is a world
order in which authority of the almighty God and the lordship
of His Son Jesus Christ are acknowledged as supreme. It is a
world order based on love and peace.

The New Testament world order—the kingdom of God—is
a three-dimensional world order in terms of time. It has a past,
a present, and a future. "Repent: for the kingdom of heaven is
at hand," said Jesus (Matt. 4:17 KJV). The kingdom came when
Jesus came. The history of the New Testament world order began with the life, death, and resurrection of Jesus Christ. "The
kingdom of God is within you," He added (Luke 17:21). The
kingdom is a *present* reality among those who have accepted
the lordship of Jesus. "Thy kingdom come," Jesus prayed (Matt.
6:10 KJV). The Lord's Prayer indicates that the kingdom of God
will fully come someday. This is the future dimension of the
kingdom of God.

The kingdom of God operates on certain principles that
are often contrary to the principles of the present world order.
Some of these principles are: love your enemies (Matt. 5:43);
live by dying (Gal. 2:20); receive by giving (Luke 6:38); gain by
losing (Matt. 10:39); be the first by being the last (Mark 10:31);
and seek the kingdom first (Matt. 6:33).

According to the apostle Paul, the kingdom of God is not
meat or drink (KJV); it is righteousness, peace, and joy in the
Holy Spirit (Rom. 14:17). In other words, it is a spiritual reality
we can be a part of now.

One should not be discouraged by the current world disorder, because beyond this disorder, unnoticed by many, is
the present reality of the kingdom of God: the church of Jesus

Christ. Through this community of faith, the kingdom of God is in operation now. People in all walks of life who have accepted Jesus Christ as their Lord and Savior are spiritual participants in the kingdom life now.

The full potential of the kingdom of God will not be realized until the coming of the Lord Jesus Christ. Until then, the church of Jesus Christ, anxiously awaiting the Lord's return, will continue to represent that world order on this earth without much fanfare.

17

PASTORAL COUNSELING
AND ALTAR MINISTRY

The term *pastoral counseling* means different things to different people. While some think of it as a purely humanistic psychological exercise, others seem to think of it as a method to beat believers with a big Bible. Pastoral counseling is neither a necessary evil to be unwillingly tolerated nor a demonic presence to be cast out of the church. Pastoral counseling, to me, is extended altar ministry.

The average churchgoer who attends all the services hears his pastor speak to him for no more than an hour and a half weekly. If he skips at least one evening service per week, his input from the pastor is even less. Now consider that the average American watches television nearly fifty hours a week. Even a person who watches no televised programs other than the evening network news hears the newscaster speak to him for two and a half hours weekly. Consider also that a lot of the recent church growth is accomplished at the expense of pastoral care—that is, pastors have less and less time to visit, pray, and engage in closer spiritual encounters with their people. These facts point out the need to have an increasing number of one-to-one meetings between the pastors and, at least, the neediest of their congregations. Pastoral counseling offers this opportunity.

People who see no difference between secular psychological counseling and pastoral counseling often raise questions about the validity of the latter in the local church. If secular humanistic counseling is only whitewashed as pastoral counseling, their questions would be valid. Their argument that the old-fashioned "praying through" is a much better approach would be acceptable. However, how many altar services in contemporary America last for hours? How many churches schedule such altar ministry? How many people will make room in their schedules for such regular events? The alternative is to schedule altar services for individuals away from the altar to meet their scheduling and privacy needs. The result will be pastoral counseling sessions.

At one time I pastored a fast-growing church in Connecticut. In my pastorate, I considered my office (study) as sacred a ground as the sanctuary itself. I wanted to see God move in my office as He did at the altar.

I see the need today for more pastors to consider their offices or study rooms as sacred as their pulpits or altars. To me, what I did in the study was only an extension of what I did at the altar. At the altar, I was in the business of healing, guiding, reconciling, and sustaining. I continued this ministry in the study too. God, who graciously moved at the altar, moved also in the study.

My model for pastoral counseling is Jesus. His dialogue with the Samaritan women at the well in John's gospel is my model of a counseling session. A dialogue about H_2O turned into a life-changing, city-changing experience. Pastoral counseling can be evangelistic! Interestingly, this encounter did not take place at the temple. Pastoral counseling can take place at the altar, in the study, or even in someone's living room.

True pastoral counseling involves insights, inspiration, and discernment. This is a skill-requiring ministry. The disciples of Jesus were trained in it for at least three and a half years. Unskilled altar ministry can cause harm. So can unskilled pastoral counseling. I have seen the results of both. But that is no reason to discredit either altar ministry or pastoral counseling.

Pastoral counseling is Spirit-led, creative dialogue that leads to prayer. True pastoral counseling leads both the pastor and his counselee to their knees. The Spirit of the living God that moves at the altar to bring healing and wholeness to individuals moves also upon those who will kneel with their pastor in his study.

18

RESPONSIBILITY
WITHOUT AUTHORITY

A common mistake made by Christian churches and ministries is to delegate responsibility without offering adequate
authority to an individual who is to fulfill it. This seems to be
a problem among Pentecostal/charismatic people in particular.
The major cause of this unhealthy situation is ignorance or
insecurity on the part of leaders.

In order to carry out a responsibility in an organization, an
individual must have the necessary amount of authority. Every
responsibility requires a corresponding degree of authority. Ministers and ministry leaders often delegate responsibilities to their
subordinates, but do not give them any authority to implement
them. The result is delay, disappointment, and disillusionment.

When Jesus sent His disciples to go into all the world, He
gave them authority to preach, teach, and heal. The disciples
went in the name of the One who said that He had all authority

in heaven and earth. The Father had given Him that authority, and He gave it to His disciples.

Jesus believed in bestowing authority. Although anyone can delegate responsibility, it takes a mature leader, who is sure of his own calling, to delegate authority. One who is fighting to keep his own chair is not capable of sharing authority.

Many leaders are afraid to give authority. They are afraid that by sharing authority they might lose their own authority. The truth is that in Christian life, giving away authority is actually the way to increase it for oneself. We must not be afraid to share authority with trustworthy people. Jesus did not diminish His authority by passing it on to His disciples.

The classic example of this issue in the charismatic churches is the behavior of many senior pastors who do not allow associates to carry out any ministerial task of significance. A good leader will allow others to grow into leadership. Moses raised up Joshua, who was capable of taking charge with little notice. Why do we often experience a leadership vacuum upon the death of older leaders? The answer may rest in the fact that many of our older leaders have not trained the younger ones by giving them responsibility with authority under supervision.

19

SEVEN TYPES
OF CHURCHES IN REVELATION

The book of Revelation presents seven churches for our consideration. There were positive statements, a list of issues, and instructions that were given to these churches. I have listed them in the essay that follows, using scriptures from the NIV. Which church best represents yours?

1. The Love-Challenged Church at Ephesus

Positives: Revelation 2:2–3, 6: "I know your deeds, your hard work and your perseverance. I know that you cannot tolerate wicked people, that you have tested those who claim to be apostles but are not, and have found them false. You have persevered and have endured hardships for my name, and have not grown weary . . . You have this in your favor: You hate the practices of the Nicolaitans, which I also hate."

Issues: Revelation 2:4: "Yet I hold this against you: You have forsaken the love you had at first."

Instructions: Revelation 2:5: "Consider how far you have fallen! Repent and do the things you did at first. If you do not repent, I will come to you and remove your lampstand from its place."

2. The Persecuted Church at Smyrna

Positives: Revelation 2:9: "I know your afflictions and your poverty—yet you are rich! I know about the slander of those who say they are Jews and are not, but are a synagogue of Satan."

Issues: None listed against the church

Instructions: Revelation 2:10: "Do not be afraid of what you are about to suffer. I tell you, the devil will put some of you in prison to test you, and you will suffer persecution for ten days. Be faithful, even to the point of death, and I will give you life as your victor's crown."

3. The Tolerant Church at Pergamum

Positives: Revelation 2:13: "I know where you live—where Satan has his throne. Yet you remain true to my name. You did not renounce your faith in me, not even in the days of Antipas, my faithful witness, who was put to death in your city—where Satan lives."

Issues: Revelation 2:14–15: "Nevertheless, I have a few things against you: There are some among you who hold to the teaching of Balaam, who taught Balak to entice the Israelites to sin so that they ate food sacrificed to idols and committed sexual immorality. Likewise you also have those who hold to the teaching of the Nicolaitans."

Instructions: Revelation 2:16: "Repent therefore! Otherwise, I will soon come to you and will fight against them with the sword of my mouth."

4. The Compromising Church at Thyatira

Positives: Revelation 2:19: "I know your deeds, your love and faith, your service and perseverance, and that you are now doing more than you did at first."

Issues: Revelation 2:20–21: "Nevertheless, I have this against you: You tolerate that woman Jezebel, who calls herself a prophet. By her teaching she misleads my servants into sexual immorality and the eating of food sacrificed to idols. I have given her time to repent of her immorality, but she is unwilling."

Warnings: Revelation 2:22–23: "So I will cast her on a bed of suffering, and I will make those who commit adultery with her suffer intensely, unless they repent of her ways. I will strike her children dead. Then all the churches will know that I am he who searches hearts and minds, and I will repay each of you according to your deeds."

5. The Dead Church at Sardis

Positives: Revelation 3:4–5: "You have a few people in Sardis who have not soiled their clothes. They will walk with me, dressed in white, for they are worthy. The one who is victorious will, like them, be dressed in white. I will never blot out the name of that person from the book of life, but will acknowledge that name before my Father and his angels."

Issues: Revelation 3:1–2: "I know your deeds; you have a reputation of being alive, but you are dead. Wake up! Strengthen what remains and is about to die, for I have found your deeds unfinished in the sight of my God."

Instructions: Revelation 3:3: "Remember, therefore, what you have received and heard; hold it fast, and repent. But if you do not wake up, I will come like a thief, and you will not know at what time I will come to you."

6. The Open-Door Church at Philadelphia

Positives: Revelation 3:8: "I know your deeds. See, I have placed before you an open door that no one can shut. I know that you have little strength, yet you have kept my word and have not denied my name."

Issues: None listed

Instructions/Promises: Revelation 3:9–12: "I will make those who are of the synagogue of Satan, who claim to be Jews though they are not, but are liars—I will make them come and fall down at your feet and acknowledge that I have loved you. Since you have kept my command to endure patiently, I will also keep you from the hour of trial that is going to come on the whole world to test the inhabitants of the earth. I am coming soon. Hold on to what you have, so that no one will take your crown. The one who is victorious I will make a pillar in the temple of my God. Never again will they leave it. I will write on them the name of my God and the name of the city of my God, the new Jerusalem, which is coming down out of heaven from my God; and I will also write on them my new name."

7. The Indifferent Church at Laodicea

Positives: None listed

Issues: Revelation 3:15–17: "I know your deeds, that you are neither cold nor hot. I wish you were either one or the other! So, because you are lukewarm—neither hot nor cold—I am about to spit you out of my mouth. You say, 'I am rich; I have acquired wealth and do not need a thing.' But you do not realize that you are wretched, pitiful, poor, blind and naked."

Instructions: Revelation 3:18: "I counsel you to buy from me gold refined in the fire, so you can become rich; and white clothes to wear, so you can cover your shameful nakedness; and salve to put on your eyes, so you can see."

20

THE CHURCH:
GOD'S GREAT PROJECT

Do you know that more than the International Monetary Fund, the great Olympic Games, and the United Nations, God is concerned about His church? Jesus gave His life for the church (Eph. 5:25), not for some bank. He has determined, "I will build my church; and the gates of hell shall not prevail against it" (Matt. 16:18 KJV). What is this great enterprise God is concerned about?

The New Testament word for *church* is *ekklesia*, which means "the assembly of those who are called." However, the word does not imply a building or a place of assembly. It is about people who are related to one another, not by being in one place, but by being connected to each other through the Head—Jesus Christ. The Bible calls the church by several names, such as the bride of Christ, the body of Christ, the temple of the Holy Spirit, family, and the household of faith.

The church is to be a different kind of community: a community of faith, transformed by the power of the Holy Spirit and not conforming to this world. Jesus' teaching on the kingdom of God is the pattern for the church. The kingdom of God follows a different order. In the kingdom, the first shall be last and the last shall be first, giving is the way to receive, and dying is the way to live! The church is to exemplify this new order by the grace of God and be a prototype of life in the community as God envisions it.

Jesus Christ is the founder of the church. His own words testify to this truth: "I will build my church." Any definition of the church must conform to the Word of God. Church is a congregation of the faithful who are called by God to join His family. They are called to be followers of Jesus of Nazareth, the Son of the living God. The church must preach the word of God and administer the ordinances. The church must facilitate worship of God and fellowship of the saints.

Members of the church are called by God. They are adopted into the family of God. They are a priesthood set apart for the purposes of God. They are to be led by the Holy Spirit. They are to be a people of faith, hope, and love.

The church has an organizational dimension, but it is truly a living organism. Any healthy living organism will grow and develop. So also the church must grow and develop. God's Word and His Spirit sustain the life of the church.

The church has been saved to serve. God uses His apostles, prophets, evangelists, pastors, and teachers for the equipping of the saints for this work of service

The church is called to worship, evangelize, fellowship, and show mercy to the needy. The last words of Jesus, according to

75

Matthew, remind us that the mission of the church is to go into *all* the world, preach to *all* nations, and teach them to obey *all* things commanded by Him. Generally speaking, the church is to continue the work of Jesus by engaging in preaching, teaching, and healing. God loves His church and gives firm warning to those who would try to destroy it. He will not allow the gates of hell to prevail against His church.

The history of the church teaches us that the blood of martyrs is the seed of the church. It teaches us that relying on human calculations to expand the church is doomed to fail. Whenever the church adopted humanistic, territorial, and political means to spread itself, it failed miserably. Church history teaches us that whenever the church failed to love people into the kingdom of God, it caused great damage to itself. Princes of state and princes of the "church" could not repair the damage. Allow the church to grow where the wind of God is blowing. Those who plant by the river of God will reap a great harvest.

The church of Jesus Christ is a community of hope. We are "hope bearers," and Christ in us is the hope of glory. Our hope is not in some date or event. Our hope is in a person—the Lord Jesus Christ, who lived, died, was buried, and rose again. He has ascended to heaven and is seated at the right hand of His Father. The hope of the church is that He will come again to receive the church. While no one knows the day or the hour of His coming, one thing is certain: "so shall we ever be with the Lord" (1 Thess. 4:17 KJV). The church lives in this eschatological hope and shares that hope with the world in word and deed.

The church is a leaven of hope in this world. It is a reminder that God has a plan for His world and that plan will be accomplished. The church is a herald, inviting people into the kingdom of God and announcing the coming of the King. The church by its very nature is a sign to the entire world that God is in our midst and that He is at work.

PART II

SPIRIT-LED MINISTRY

21

WHAT IS SPIRIT-LED MINISTRY?

Someone asked me to explain what Spirit-led ministry is for people who are not professional preachers, seminarians, or Bible school students. In this brief article, I would like to respond to that request.

Spirit-led ministry is the life and service of a man or woman who is called by God to represent Him and the good news of Jesus Christ in this world. It is the lifestyle and practices of servants of God who consider themselves disciples of Jesus Christ. It is the life of service of called individuals who are filled with the Holy Spirit and are open to and responsive to the promptings of the Spirit on an ongoing basis.

Spirit-led ministry may involve words and actions; words are not necessarily required, but prayer is always involved. A Spirit-led minister is a person of prayer and a student of the Word of God.

A Spirit-led minister communicates the gospel of Jesus Christ using all available means. It may be through preaching and teaching or some other means of communication. A Spirit-led minister will depend on the power of the Holy Spirit to enhance this effort to communicate.

A Spirit-led minister is one who is concerned about the welfare of others, especially those who are in distress or pain. This is a person whose heart breaks for the things that break God's heart. It is someone who gives oneself in the service of God and for the advancement of God's agenda in the world, an ambassador of reconciliation between people and people and between people and God.

Spirit-led ministers are concerned about the brokenness of the world and willing to offer themselves to minister healing and wholeness in the name of Jesus. They are concerned about individuals, families, and communities, seeing themselves as members of God's family and citizens of God's kingdom.

Spirit-led ministers are servant leaders who look to the Holy Spirit for empowerment and strength. They are willing to submit their gifts and talents to God for His purposes and know that God can use even their weaknesses and inabilities. They do not boss people around or use them for personal goals, but invest in them for their growth and development to accomplish common goals.

A Spirit-led minister is a person of faith and hope, and a symbol of hope to those in despair. This person cares for others and is concerned about them. A Spirit-led minister lives with the awareness of one's own mortality, and with a humble assurance of one day being called a "faithful servant."

22

FAITH AND POWER IN MINISTRY

A s noted in previous articles, I am a third-generation minister. I was born and raised in a parsonage in India. My father and grandfather were local pastors. My father pastored his last congregation for more than thirty years! He was my pastor, teacher, baptizer, and mentor until I left home to go to seminary in the United States. I have been a pastor, chaplain, and seminary professor since then. I have been a part of an international healing and educational ministry for thirty-five years. I also have been fortunate to gain extensive experience in short-term ministry internationally. I have said all this to claim that I have been a participant observer of Pentecostal/charismatic ministry from different perspectives and in different contexts for over half a century.

I can make several statements about ministry based on my own observations and convictions. I want to share two such statements here. First, ministry can be done with faith or without faith. It is better to do it by faith. Second, ministry can be done by one's own strength or in the strength of the Holy Spirit. It is better to depend on the Holy Spirit's strength.

Although we give lip service to the idea of doing ministry by faith, many ministers do not practice what they say. They will make statements of faith, but when it is time to make decisions, they often fall back on personal calculations. I am not talking about counting the cost before building, as Jesus suggested (Luke 14:28), but of counting the obstacles to what God had told them to do. This, of course, is not a new problem. We see this even during the time of Jesus.

Remember the feeding of the five thousand? Jesus had compassion on the multitude that had been listening to Him for a long time. He felt their hunger and wanted to help them. He commanded His disciples to feed the multitude. Can you imagine Jesus asking them to do something He thought they could not do? He had a plan. But how did the disciples respond? Listen to Philip. He did some fast calculations and concluded that it would take eight months of wages to give the crowd a bite of food each. Does this sound like faith to you? How often are we just like Philip? Full of faith apparently, but not fully grasping God's plan or really believing His Word.

Now think of the apostle to India, Saint Thomas. He is of special interest to me because God used this cautious disciple to bring the gospel to India. In my estimate, Indians are the most genetically unbelieving people. Maybe it has to do with the fact that they have a history of more than five thousand years and they have been manipulated by so many religions. In fact, the typical Hindu has to choose between 330 million gods. That is nearly one god per three Indians. They don't want to be deceived by another god. God in His wisdom chose to send a doubter like Thomas to India. Thank God, Christianity has survived two thousand years in India, and in many ways it is thriving now, although it cannot be compared to countries like South Korea. Then again, in India one is not dealing with a smaller, monocultural group of people, like the Koreans. India is an unbelievable mix of more than a billion people!

The best-case example of Thomas as a devoted doubter is the incident of the raising of Lazarus from the dead. Jesus told His disciples that He was going to Bethany to raise Lazarus from the dead. He left no doubt that His goal was to raise the dead man. Thomas actually volunteered to go with Jesus. He loved Jesus and believed in Jesus, but in terms of the goal for going, Thomas had a hard time believing it. He said to his peers, "Let us also go and die with Jesus" (John 11:15, paraphrased).

He not only was expecting Lazarus to remain dead; he expected Jesus and himself to be killed by the end of the adventure! Do you see the problem? Thomas was ministering without believing. Of course, we know that before going to India, Thomas had to settle the issue with Jesus in a very personal encounter. Who can forget how he cried out, "My Lord and My God!" when he saw the nail holes in Jesus' hands and feet (John 20:28)? Once and for all, Thomas decided who Jesus was. He believed and, by faith, went to India, where, according to many traditions, he died a martyr's death.

When I think of faith to accomplish something for God, I often think of the Old Testament saint Caleb. He disagreed with the majority report of the spies Moses sent to check out the land of promise. They said that the land was fine, but they were not able to possess it because there were giants living there. They felt they were like grasshoppers! The giant grapes they brought from the Promised Land were right there before them as they spoke, but the unbelievers focused on the giants that may or may not have existed, rather than on the grapes that were a testimony of God's plan to provide for them.

Caleb chose to keep his eyes on the grapes, not on the giants. He declared that they were "well able" to possess the land (Num. 13:30). That was faith. Faith in action. He had no more information than the others, but he had a different perspective—a perspective of faith.

That is my point. We can minister like Philip or Thomas, or we can minister like Caleb. It is indeed better to minister like Caleb. It is better to minister by faith. I heard a definition of faith some time ago. I don't know who the author is, but I really like it: *Faith sees the invisible. Faith believes the incredible. Faith accomplishes the impossible!* Faith—what a simple, yet profound, idea!

Now, the issue of power in ministry: Here again, ministers are tempted to depend on their own gifts and talents alone rather than the Holy Spirit. This is a strong temptation because it is very easy to fall back on one's own abilities instead of waiting on the Lord. One's gifts become the constant default drive for ministry, so to speak.

People who minister out of their own resources alone burn out very fast. Burnout is the result of giving to others without receiving. Ministry requires a lifestyle of giving *and* receiving spiritual nourishment. Depending on the Holy Spirit means one will never run out of spiritual resources. Depending only on one's own personal gifts and talents limits the impact of one's ministry. A charismatic personality is no substitute for a truly charismatic ministry—a ministry led by the Spirit, the giver of *charisms* (gifts).

A story that helps me understand this best comes from Australia, where David Huxley won an unusual competition. He won first place and beat his own previous record by pulling a Boeing 747 jumbo jet one hundred yards in just over one minute. He tied a steel rope from the front wheel of the plane to himself and pulled the 189-ton machine! What a feat! Of course, when the competition was over, Mr. Huxley was completely exhausted. Good accomplishment, but a bad idea to imitate.

An airliner is not designed to be pulled. It is designed to fly. Ministry without dependence on the Holy Spirit is basically like pulling an airliner created to fly. A Boeing 747 can fly from continent to continent. It can stay in the sky for hours. If Mr. Huxley could get inside the plane and have a pilot fly the machine, he could get farther and arrive much less exhausted.

In ministry, we are called to fly under the wings of the Holy Spirit. No wonder Jesus told His disciples to wait in the city until they received power from above before they ventured out of Jerusalem to the uttermost parts of the earth (Acts 1:4).

Yes, we can minister by faith or without faith. My advice is, minister by faith. We can minister with the empowerment of the Holy Spirit or by depending only on our own gifting. It is much better to depend on the Holy Spirit! Have a great flight!

23

BIBLICAL QUALITIES
OF A GOOD LEADER

At the beginning of a certain school year, I began to prepare a message to share with the faculty at the ORU School of
Theology and Ministry. I felt led to talk to them about Christian leadership. I wanted them to see themselves as more than
professors or academic professionals; my goal was to help them
view themselves as leaders, and to see their work at the seminary as leadership training. After all, as a seminary, we are in
the business of training leaders for the Pentecostal/Charismatic
movement of the twenty-first century.

Books on the subject of leadership are plentiful on the
market today. Although both secular and Christian books on
this topic abound, I wanted to look for a leader in the Bible for
my study and presentation. Naturally, Moses was the first name
that came to my mind.

Moses was certainly a leader of God's people; God Himself
chose him. In reviewing Moses' life and ministry, I was able

to see eight distinctive leadership characteristics in him. I will simply list them in this article.

1. The ability to hear God. Moses was a man who had an ear for God's voice. From the time he heard the voice coming out of the burning bush, Moses always wanted to hear God. Even when God's message was stern, Moses listened to it carefully.

2. A commitment to obeying God. It is one thing to listen to God, but quite another to obey him. Moses was an obedient servant of God. Except for a rare occasion, Moses followed God's directives very closely. He stood for God and implemented His wishes among the people. People often disliked it, but Moses gave priority to God's opinion of him.

3. The courage to confront evil. Moses was not afraid to confront evil. He was willing to look the oppressor in the face and command him to let God's people go. Human power did not intimidate this man of God. He knew that the Egyptian leader could destroy his body, but not his spirit.

4. The mettle to correct the saints. Moses was willing to correct the saints when they needed correction. He rebuked them and disciplined them as needed. He knew that he served a holy God, and he wanted his people to please God.

5. A willingness to intercede for the people. Moses could be a rough disciplinarian, but he was a caring shepherd in his heart. Moses was a prophet and priest at the same time. As prophet, he told them, "Thus saith the LORD;" as priest, he cried out before God on behalf of his people. He stood in the gap for them.

6. A resolve to remain human. Many leaders try to act as if they are different from their people. Some act in a spiritually superior way, as if they have a secret connection to God that others do not have. Most of them are faking it. Moses was a man of God, but in the presence of his people he remained human. The glory of God was on his face, but he lived his daily life before them as a human being. He was happy, sad, and angry, like any other human being, but he was their leader. He knew his position, and the people accepted it.

7. *A readiness to mentor others.* Many leaders are so self-absorbed and shortsighted that they act as if they will be present to lead the people forever. Moses was different. He mentored others in leadership, and trained them to take their roles as leaders in the future. He wanted to make sure there would never be a leadership vacuum upon his death. Our organizations today experience a leadership vacuum quite often because people are not mentored to take these positions.

8. *The willingness to delegate authority to anointed leaders.* Moses shared responsibility and authority with others. He allowed them to assist him in his work and trained them for future responsibilities in the process. When the time came, there was a Joshua to take his place in leadership. Joshua was not overwhelmed because he was properly trained through mentoring and delegation of authority.

I believe these qualities are important for all Christian leaders, whether they are professors or pastors. Although we have plenty of office holders, there is a great shortage of good leaders among us today. A corrupt political process will not produce this type of leaders; only a biblical model of leadership training can accomplish such a task. I pray for a harvest of leaders among our people. May these qualities be found in them.

24

GOD CAN USE YOUR WEAKNESSES!

Henri Nouwen was professor of pastoral care at Yale University Divinity School when I was a student there three decades ago. His best-known work is titled *The Wounded Healer*. The thesis of this book is this: Jesus Christ is the true wounded Healer. By His stripes we are healed. God can use wounded Christians who are in the process of being healed to minister healing to hurting people around them.

Henri Nouwen's idea about the wounded healer is not very well-known among Pentecostals and charismatics. We often project an image that God can use only the strong. We act as if God uses only our strengths. Yes, God does use our strengths, but He is not limited to using only our strengths.

Because of the false idea that God can only use strong and talented people for His purposes, many Christians choose to remain totally inactive in God's work. This is a great loss.

What does the Bible say about this matter? The apostle Paul is a strong witness in support of the idea that God works through us in spite of our weaknesses. He talked about his own thorn in his flesh (2 Cor. 12:7–9). Whatever it was, one thing is clear. God told him that His grace was sufficient for him. The lesson Paul learned was that God's strength can be made perfect in our weaknesses. In other words, God reveals His strength through our weaknesses and accomplishes His purposes.

By weakness, I do not mean constant moral failures. I am speaking of inabilities and inadequacies all of us experience in life. It may also mean a situational difficulty or some form of handicap.

Look at the history of God's people. Have you considered the unlikely people God has used, and their weaknesses? Here is a partial list: Abraham was too old. Moses stuttered. Timothy had stomach problems. Rahab was a prostitute. Amos only knew farming. Thomas was a doubter. Peter had a fast temper. The list can go on and on. The fact is that God used all these people in spite of their issues.

I remember the words of Dean Collin Williams at Yale Divinity School long ago. He stated that the degrees we were earning were only like the five loaves of bread in the hands of a lad. They could not feed the hungry crowd, but if we would give them to Jesus, He would bless them, break them, and multiply them to feed the multitude!

Please don't be discouraged because someone else has more skills and talents than you have. Give your strengths as well as your weaknesses to God, and ask Him to use them for His glory. He will take them in His hands, break them, bless them, and use them for His purposes. What matters is your surrender to God. He will begin with your brokenness and make everything beautiful in His time.

25

THEOLOGICAL REFLECTION: A NEEDED DISCIPLINE

A very old man and an infant are brought to a hospital at the same time with a severe asthma attack. Both need assistance in breathing, but the hospital has only one respiratory machine (artificial breathing machine). You are the doctor who must decide who gets the only machine available. To whom will you give the machine: to the infant, who has her whole life ahead of her; or to the old man, who has lived a long time already? How will you make that decision as a Spirit-filled Christian?

A rich man, who has several living children, leaves a number of artificially created embryos behind in frozen condition for future development. He dies. His wife wants to develop the embryos into children after the man has been dead for a time. Should she be allowed to do so, or should the embryos be killed or destroyed? The living children will have to share their inheritance with the children to be developed from the embryos.

In modern society, women who want to terminate a pregnancy no longer need a surgical procedure to do so. They can take a pill that is legally available in several countries and have a chemically induced abortion. Should that be allowed? Is that the right thing to do?

A cancer patient cannot take the pain of the disease anymore. A doctor is willing to assist her to commit suicide to avoid the pain. Should he be allowed to do so? If you are an attending doctor or nurse, how should you respond to the physician offering assisted suicide?

These are not hypothetical situations anymore; they are real-life situations brought to us by fast-exploding modern technology. The same modern science that brought us satellite communication and multimedia entertainment has also created these very difficult ethical dilemmas. How should we respond to these situations as Spirit-led Christians, and how should we make decisions regarding these issues?

There was a time when we could look for a proof text (verse) from the Bible to provide the answer. The Word of God is still the same; it still has the answers to all human situations, but we no longer have the luxury of proof texting or simply finding a verse as the answer to many complex situations. For instance, the Bible does not directly say, "Thou shalt not watch MTV" (vulgar music television) or "Thou shalt not perform assisted suicide," or "Thou shalt not smoke cigars."

There are still many Christians, particularly Pentecostals, who insist that proof texting is the answer to all problems. They will often take verses out of context and try to argue their points. Although there are plenty of clear directives and commands given in God's Word, many of the dilemmas facing modern believers come in very subtle and complex forms. Simplistic solutions will not answer the issues clearly. What should we do then?

This is where the discipline of theological reflection comes in. Theological reflection is the spiritual discipline of looking at any experience or cultural situation through the prism of the Word of God, illuminated by the Holy Spirit, who is working within the history, tradition, and boundaries of a community of faith, which is the church of Jesus Christ. This is a fancy way to say that in order to know what to do in very difficult and unclear situations, we must seek the teaching of the Word of God and the guidance of the Holy Spirit, who is always at work in the body of Christ. In other words, we should not simply look for verses to quote in every situation, but rather we should be listening to the principles and wholesome directives of the Word of God that can assist us in making decisions that would please the Lord.

God has not left us alone. He has promised to be with us. He is the living Word among us, who has given us the written Word. He has also made us members of His body, where we can depend on one another. Therefore, instead of proof texting in isolation, we must seek the will of God in prayer, reflection, and meditation. God will reveal His will to us through the Word of God, the Spirit of God, and the people of God.

People who act as though they have the answers to all the problems of the world cannot carry out theological reflection well; it is for those who have a humble spirit. This practice is also not for the impatient; it takes time to know the will of God. To do this well, one must study the Word of God regularly and know what is in the written Word. Only those who know what is in the written word can find words, metaphors, images, and, directives to inform and guide them in the decision-making process.

The Word of God answers some issues directly; however, answers to many modern dilemmas must be discerned through theological reflection. There are times when the answer must be received in a hurry. On such occasions, the Holy Spirit can empower us through the gifts of the Spirit, such as word of wisdom and word of knowledge. There are certain historic Christian churches that claim a long history of practicing theological reflection. They seldom brag about being filled with the Holy Spirit. At the same time, although Pentecostals claim a Spirit-filled life, when it comes to the discipline of theological reflection, we are far behind our traditional brothers. This is not the Holy Spirit's fault; we are the problem. We are the ones who need the disciplines of study, prayer, reflection, and meditation. If historic churches with a lesser emphasis on the current work of the Holy Spirit can develop the discipline of theological reflection, how much more could we who are filled with the Spirit allow the Spirit to illuminate our hearts and minds?

It is time for Spirit-filled Christians to stop looking for out-of-context verses to answer complicated questions posed to us by modern civilization. Instead, we must reflect on God's Word, as led by the Holy Spirit, to discover the divine solutions to the challenging issues that are facing us today.

26

CAREFRONTATION:
SPEAKING TRUTH IN LOVE

"Carefrontation" is a new term that has been coined by professionals in the field of Christian counseling. The term is a softer variation of the word *confrontation,* which has a stronger connotation. Carefrontation is defined as caring enough to confront gently or caring enough to tell the truth in love.

Speaking the truth in love is a biblical idea. "Instead, speaking the truth in love, we will grow to become in every respect the mature body of him who is the head" (Eph. 4:15 NIV). This idea is not very popular in our community today. I am not suggesting that we have many liars among us or that we do not believe in truth anymore. I am referring to the issue of speaking out. Many who know the truth prefer not to speak it, and they certainly do not wish to write it. I am sympathetic to them because I know from experience that speaking the truth can cost you dearly. I have personally experienced paying the price for speaking out.

I know there are others who observe the same things I do and have the same insights about their observations. There are those who know what is wrong and what should be done about improving certain situations, but they are unable, unwilling, or afraid to speak it. They do not want to take the heat for it from those who are responsible for the problems or who benefit from the status quo.

At times, I too am tempted to avoid speaking the truth and to just mind my own business and look the other way, while the suffering, poor performance, or injustice continues. But deep inside I believe that I have a moral obligation to speak the truth.

The Bible requires more than just speaking the truth—it demands that it be done in love. This is another problem area in our community. Those who speak the truth seem to do it so harshly that those who need to listen to the truth are unable to hear it clearly or accept it fully because it is shared in such hostile fashion.

This is especially true of some among us who may have what is considered a prophetic ministry. These individuals may have insights about a situation. They may know the truth and may even speak it, but they speak it in such a threatening fashion that the recipient of this message is unable to accept it and respond to it.

Why does the Bible require that we speak the truth in love? I believe it is because God knows that truth is painful enough and that if it is given without love, we are unable to accept it. Truth is like bitter medicine; some sugar will make it easier for the patient to swallow it. The expression of love is the sugar that makes the truth go down more easily.

Someone has defined the word *therapy* this way: therapy is telling the truth to someone in such a way that she or he can receive the truth about herself or himself. Accepting the truth about a situation is important for one's health and well-being; but someone must care enough to speak truth to us before we can accept it. This applies to individuals and communities.

Imagine that a friend comes to your office after lunch with some food crumbs prominently stuck to the side of his mouth. You could act as if you don't see it, or you could insult him for being a careless slob who keeps his face loaded with leftover food. The other option would be to kindly tell the person about the crumbs on his face and to help him take care of it. The situation is the same even when the observation is not as easily visible as the food on one's face. Truthful words help a person do something about his or her situation. Insulting someone is generally not helpful, even when the words are delivered in the form of a spiritual prophecy.

I can think of people who helped me by speaking truth to me about myself in a loving way. There were times that I felt uncomfortable or embarrassed when I first heard it; however, in the long run, I have benefited from truths spoken to me. I am convinced that only truth can set a person free and that we must be open to truth even when it hurts. At the same time, we must learn to speak truth lovingly. The fact that we have a ministry of prophecy or a position of authority does not give us the right to speak truth unlovingly. We must learn to speak truth in love.

Speaking truth is a risky business. Whenever one speaks the truth, one risks the rejection of that truth, and even of oneself. This is a chance we must take. Some of us are too safety conscious and do not risk speaking the truth. I believe we deprive others of their potential for excellence by not speaking the truth.

Truth must not be assumed. Everything that looks like truth is not truth. Truth is that which passes the test of truthfulness. We must make sure that what we consider truth is indeed true. The Word of God is the ultimate truth; therefore, anything we consider truthful should pass the test of the inspired word. We must make sure that the Scripture supports our position and our teachings. If something is true according to the Bible, we should not be afraid to speak it.

There were times that I had to take some heat for speaking the truth. But in the long run, I have been grateful for the outcome of speaking truth in love. At the same time, speaking the truth in an unloving way has backfired on me on several occasions. So, friends, do not close your eyes to truth. Do not be afraid of the consequences of speaking the truth. Speak the truth; write the truth. Always do so in love.

Carefrontation is caring enough to confront. This is what God did through Jesus Christ.

27

THE SACRED VOCATION OF PASTOR

The autobiographical book *The Pastor: A Memoir* by Eugene H. Peterson,[9] the pastor who authored the *Message* version of the Bible, articulated the vocation of pastor in a very moving way. Born to a butcher father and Pentecostal preacher mother, Peterson was lured away by God's call from a prestigious academic life as professor to become a pastor of a local church. In his vivid description of that journey, Peterson makes many vital observations that are very important for contemporary pastors who are highly tempted to go for the glitter and glory of unbiblical leadership models and professional performance.

The current culture demands leaders who can "get things done" and "make things happen." Bible colleges and seminaries are guilty of buying into this idea without critique. Christian media are also guilty as they promote performers rather than true pastors. Certainly, pastors must also be doers, but according to Peterson, if pastoring is reduced to simply performance,

---

9 Eugene H. Peterson, *The Pastor: A Memoir* (New York: HarperOne, 2011).

we are losing the essential element of being a pastor, which is to watch over the souls of men and women, to care for them, and to pray without ceasing.[10]

Pastors are not created by seminaries; God makes pastors. It is the call of God that makes a pastor. We have some people now in pastoral positions because they have certain skills, but having no pastoral calling, they wind up making the congregation of the people of God their "audience" and "marketplace."

Personally, I do not believe that there is anything wrong with adapting useful ideas about organization, leadership, or communication for the sake of the gospel. The problem is accepting them without biblical scrutiny and adopting those that are contrary to the spirit of the Word of God just because they "work." I am not suggesting that we abandon all methodologies of ministry just because they are not directly mentioned in the Bible. What I am saying, as Peterson has so eloquently done in his volume, is to go by the Word of God. Peterson is right. Pastors are not called to be bureaucrats. Their main job is not management.[11] Primarily they are shepherds who pay attention in the name of Jesus to people who live their lives in these perilous times.

Churches are meant to grow naturally because they are living organisms. This growth is supposed to happen through conversion of people in response to the body of Christ bearing witness to the transforming power of the gospel. Stealing sheep as the mode of church growth is not biblical. Churches are not supposed to be in competition with one another, fighting for a fair share of the religious market.

---

10 Peterson, 5.
11 Peterson, 8.

Peterson makes many other interesting observations. Churches are not franchises, he says. Pastors must preach the word that their people need to hear, not just preach about the "furniture in heaven and the temperature of hell."[12] Jesus Christ and Him crucified should be our topic.

Peterson is very hard on the modern church growth movement. He may be overstating the case, but his warning that there are three intoxicators that tempt pastors—wine, women, and crowd—is very interesting. He feels that "crowds are a worse danger" because "size is the great depersonalizer."[13] Peterson is calling the church to return from the entertainment business back to the edification work.

Pastors should not be control freaks. They should not manipulate people. They must care for the people and do all they can to create a "culture of hospitality" in their churches.[14] The church should be a place where relationships are primary, a place of hospitality. Pastors must live with the awareness of their own mortality. They die daily, but also live daily with the anticipation of the resurrection. "We practice our death by giving up our will to live on our own terms. Only in that . . . are we able to practice resurrection," says Peterson.[15]

Reading Eugene Peterson's memoir brought back many memories of my own parents and grandparents. They toiled in the hills and plains of Kerala, India; finished their work; and went home to be with Christ. Informed by the Word of God and nothing much more, they lived out their vocation of being shepherds to people of modest means. They loved them and

---

12 Peterson, 216.
13 Peterson, 157, 158.
14 Peterson, 246.
15 Peterson, 290.

cared for them. They extended their own lives and resources unselfishly to hurting people for the sake of the kingdom of God. That model of pastoral ministry scared me as a child, but also drew my attention. Having been a pastor and teacher, I now recognize more fully the importance of what I saw as a child in my family of shepherds.

28

WE ARE ALL MISSIONARIES

God the Father is a missionary. God the Son is also a missionary. So is God the Holy Spirit. As the Father sent the Son, so the Son has sent us into the world.

Missionary work is no longer the domain of Westerners. It does not belong to just a few selected people anymore. Evangelization of the world is the responsibility of every disciple of Jesus. All of us are called and empowered to be carriers of the good news of Jesus Christ.

Evangelization belongs to men *and* women. The world desperately needs women missionaries. There are five hundred million Muslim women in the world who need to hear the good news. They are prohibited from dealing with men. Only women will get to relate to them. There is a reason why the prophet Joel said that "your sons and daughters will prophesy" (Joel 2:28 NIV). Our daughters must join our sons and declare the Word of the Lord to this generation. They must share the gospel in word and deed.

The evangelization of the world will not be accomplished by full-time Christian workers. Believers from all walks of life will be required to fulfill God's purposes in these last days. The Great Commission is not the great suggestion. It is a mandate for all of us.

David Shibley, a missionary evangelist who is active in Asian nations, talks about this in one of his books. According to him, each believer needs five things to accomplish God's purposes for the world: (1) a global worldview, (2) an open mind, (3) a clear understanding of the gospel of salvation, (4) a Pentecostal experience, and (5) a noticeably different Christian lifestyle. In other words, Shibley is calling us to return to our roots. He is calling us to repentance because the world needs a church that is apostolic, Spirit-led, and that is the light of the world.

It is time for all faith groups that agree on major doctrines to cooperate on efforts to evangelize the world. Building organizations or facilities is not a substitute for evangelization. God called a people in the Old Testament and prepared the world for the Savior. In the New Testament, God sent His Son into the world. The Father and the Son sent the Spirit to empower the church to go and make disciples. But will the church go?

We are all missionaries. We should not wait for others to do our part anymore. We must go ourselves. We must go to the nations. We must go to people groups near and far. We must go to the rich and to the poor. We must go with the mind of Christ (Phil. 2:5), the word of Christ (Col. 3:16), and the peace of God in our hearts (Phil. 4:7). We must go.

We must forsake our national and cultural superiority complexes and go. We must go indebted to Jesus, empowered by the Spirit, and compelled by God's love. The love of God that is shed abroad in our hearts must overflow to the world. This is what the Spirit is saying through many to the church today.

We are pilgrims and aliens in this world. Pilgrims are identified not by the country through which they travel, but by the country of their destination. We seek a city whose builder and maker is God. We are the salt of the earth and the light of the world. We have been called to be sent. We are a family, a body, and a community of faith. We are the people of God, called to bear witness to the power of Christ. Our testimony must get outside the four walls of our churches. We must go to Jerusalem, Judea, Samaria, and to the uttermost parts of the earth.

Truly, we are *all* called to be missionaries!

29

THE PENTECOSTAL WAY OF INTERPRETING THE BIBLE

Have you noticed the way a particular scripture verse is used to establish opposing theological positions? Whether it is about tithing or wearing ornaments, verses are often interpreted in multiple ways. Consider the major doctrines. For instance, have you noticed that non-Pentecostals and Pentecostals come to differing positions on the baptism of the Holy Spirit while basing their theologies on the very same biblical texts? What you are seeing is the difference in biblical interpretation. The text may be the same, but the ultimate meaning of any text is based on the way it is interpreted.

There are right and wrong ways of interpreting a biblical text. You may be surprised to know that some of the favorite theological beliefs among God-fearing Christians are based on irresponsible interpretations of biblical texts. Preachers and teachers of the Bible must take their work of interpretation very seriously, because wrong interpretations lead to wrong doctrines, and wrong doctrines affect people's lives in this world and the next.

It appears to me that while untrained preachers often interpret biblical texts poorly, pastors trained in Bible schools and seminaries sponsored by non-Pentecostal or anti-Pentecostal groups seem to interpret the texts often in non-Pentecostal ways. Many don't seem to understand that they are using methods of biblical interpretation that led the founders and professors of these schools to non-Pentecostal or anti-Pentecostal theological positions in the first place. Preaching based on non-Pentecostal ways of interpreting the Bible is impacting Pentecostal congregations in very negative ways.

For instance, the main aim of evangelical approaches to Bible interpretation is to find the historical meaning of particular texts. This is, of course, a very important goal. But what the text meant to someone in the original readership should not be the only concern of the Pentecostal interpreter. What the Holy Spirit is saying through the same text to current believers should also be a concern for Spirit-filled interpreters, because Pentecostals believe that the Spirit of God is actively at work in the world today, revealing God's Word and ways to humankind, especially through His church. Why should Pentecostals adopt a method of interpreting the Bible that has led others to the conclusion that the gifts of the Spirit have ceased operating?

Pentecostal interpreters of the Bible are not just passive readers. They are people who are actively engaged in discovering the meaning of the Word of God by allowing the Spirit to move within them and interact between them and the text. The Spirit illuminates the Word, giving the interpreters not only important historical understanding, but also fresh insights and revelations! The readers and hearers of the Bible need not know just the historical meaning of biblical passages; they also need to grasp the meaningfulness of the text "in the now."

Early Pentecostal interpreters and preachers were not stuck on the historical meaning of what they read in the Bible; they were looking for the meaning of the text in their contexts. This is a valid way to interpret the Bible. Scripture does more than inform us; it also transforms. Inspired interpretation that is faithful to the historical context and illuminated by the Spirit is what transforms life profoundly, not just historical meaning of texts.

Reading the Bible should not only lead to knowing about God; it should also give an opportunity to know God and hear His word. Pentecostal teachers, preachers, and other interpreters should be mindful of this. The Holy Spirit reveals God to us through His Son, Jesus Christ. Interpreters and other readers should ask, "What is the Spirit saying to us through a particular text now?"

Is this not too subjective? Can't people misunderstand what the Spirit is saying? How would you prevent false doctrines from developing from personal interpretations and claims? These are good questions, but this is where the importance of the community of faith comes in. God has His word, His Spirit, and His community to discern and guard the truth. It is the job of the Spirit-filled community to test the interpretation for witness and to keep the doctrines in balance. What else should we conclude from the words of the apostle Peter, "It seemed good to the Holy Spirit and to us . . ." (Acts 15:28 NIV)?

30

FOOLISHNESS OF PREACHING, OR FOOLISH PREACHING?

When God decided long ago to save the world through the foolishness of preaching, He was not endorsing foolish preaching. Although the Charismatic movement can rightfully claim a great number of outstanding preachers, the movement hosts more than its share of *foolish* preaching. God will save the world through preaching, but unless we improve the quality of preaching within the Charismatic movement—the human aspects of preaching that we can improve—God's work of salvation and sanctification will suffer slow progress.

We are living at a time when revolutionary changes are taking place in the field of communication. In fact, we are eyewitnesses of a great paradigm shift. Just as the invention of the printing press propelled the world from a scribal model of limited communication into the possibilities of the printed page, today we are leaping out of the printed page into the limitless digital world. We are no longer the auditory generation, reading printed matter and actively listening to spoken words; we have become a passive and demanding multimedia generation. With computers invading our lives and pushing us ahead on the information superhighway, we cannot act as if there is only one way—the old, oral way—to communicate. How do we preach to a generation of multimedia consumers in the twenty-first century?

The Unchangeable Aspects

It does not matter how much the world might change; some things about preaching should never change. Preaching is a divine-human activity. The divine aspects of preaching are unchangeable. The preacher is to proclaim the eternal Word of God. The message of preaching can never change. The Word of God is a saving word. It is a healing word, a transforming word, a word that brings conviction to sinners and demands holiness from believers. God's Word is a sanctifying word. It does not change.

The fact that preaching is an incarnational activity is also unchanging. We know what incarnation was. In incarnation the Word became flesh in Jesus and lived among us. Today, Christ in us is the hope of glory. We carry Christ in us through His Spirit, thereby becoming an incarnational presence of God in the world. In the preaching of the eternal Word, the preacher participates in God's incarnational activity in the world. There is only one Jesus, one Son of God and Savior of the world. The preacher proclaims the good news of God's saving work in and through Jesus Christ. As a person transformed by the very Word that he proclaims, the preacher is a participant in the ongoing, saving work of God.

Another aspect of preaching that does not change is the work of the Holy Spirit. The preacher can never bring conviction to his listeners, as it is the work of the Holy Spirit to convict sinners. Preachers may pour out condemnation on their listeners, but it is no substitute for the conviction that the Holy Spirit brings. Conviction leads to repentance and salvation. Condemnation does not lead to repentance. The work of the Holy Spirit is not something the preacher can control or manipulate. The preacher must let God be God and allow the Spirit of God to do His work. This is not negotiable.

The Human Aspects

The human aspects of preaching are different. They can be changed and often need to change. The poor quality of preaching is not God's fault; it's the preachers'. Let me list four areas where preachers can improve:

1. Understanding: Preachers need a fresh understanding of what preaching is supposed to be. Preaching is not a running commentary on a text or an explanatory treatment of a topic. Preaching involves announcement, instruction, testimony, and proclamation. It has pattern and purpose. A good preacher will find the Holy Spirit's purpose in the text he is working with. Through the preaching of the text, he purposes to lead nonbelievers to Christ and help Christians mature. Converts become disciples as the preacher offers instruction, exhortation, edification, and comfort. Preaching is more than information sharing. Preaching must inform and form. It must convince the hearers and persuade them to take positive actions.

A good sermon is born in the heart and mind of the preacher. It results from prayerful, reflective thinking about a chosen text as it applies to a particular context. The text has its context. So does the sermon. A good sermon is centered in Jesus Christ and delivered to a particular people. It is designed to motivate the hearers to take action.

Preaching is relational. The preacher, the hearers, the Word of God, and the Holy Spirit are involved in this relational activity. The Holy Spirit is actively involved in preaching as He enables the preacher to receive the message from God and deliver it faithfully. The same Spirit is preparing the hearts and ears of the listeners. As a relational activity, preaching is interactive. The preacher and the listeners are interacting with the Word of God as each is led by the Holy Spirit.

Preaching is an event in time and space. It is more than retelling something that happened long ago; it provides an opportunity for God to do something new, here and now. The preacher must recognize that the Holy Spirit is at work when he preaches and allow the Spirit to move the way He pleases.

2. Study: The preacher must study the Word of God before he preaches it. Starting with a verse and then launching into some travelogue or storytelling is not what God had in mind when He instructed us to preach the Word! Study the Word first. Be sure of what you are preaching. People need to hear a sure word in these unsure days. A preacher who skims the surface of a passage or overly spiritualizes a text will not be able to offer an assuring message. Before a text is preached, the preacher must be sure of its background, the people in or related to it, and its meaning to its original readers. Then only can one be sure of the message it contains for the listeners today.

We all know that the same verse can be used to support opposing doctrines. The difference is in the method of interpretation used. A preacher must have a sound hermeneutical method of interpretation. Good interpretation does not allow the preacher to impose his personal ideas onto the text. A true preacher always begins with the text and goes wherever the text takes him. I know one biblical scholar who tells his students that a text without a context is a pretext. Good interpretation always begins with the context of the text.

Preachers who neglect their homework harm their listeners. There are times when God may prompt the preacher to preach a different topic or message than the one he prepared, but this is no excuse to wait for the last minute to seek God's Word for the hour. If feeding is the biblical image of preaching, then cooking— studying the Word—must become a prerequisite of preaching. Studying is the way a preacher cooks.

Prayerful study is also the way the preacher prepares his mind to preach. God is not glorified in mindless preaching. We are led by the Spirit, but being led by the Spirit does not mean ignoring the mind. Jesus did not die on the cross to wash away our brains. He died to save us from sin and then to transform us through the renewing of our minds. A carnal Christian exposed to mindless preaching will have an untransformed mind. He will conform to this world and not even know it. We do not lean on our own understanding, but we do pray in the Spirit and with understanding! We sing in the Spirit and with understanding! We may also have to prepare and preach in the Spirit and with understanding!

3. Communication: Preachers must be constantly looking for ways to more effectively communicate the vital message they have been given. One's delivery must match one's context. Although the simplicity of the gospel should be maintained in all contexts, one's delivery must match the context and culture of the congregation. Paul preached one way in the synagogues and another way on Mars Hill (the Areopagus). His message was basically the same, but his audiences and their cultures were different. He analyzed his context! In other words, a preacher not only should exegete the *Word*; he also must exegete the *world*!

Preachers must recognize that due to the availability of Christian literature and the internet, their hearers are well-informed on many subjects. Today's preachers need more general knowledge than their predecessors. The internet is a source of information, but it can be a snare in the area of humor. What the preacher considers a fresh joke obtained online may be fresh only to him or her.

Even experienced preachers can be stuck on a particular method of delivery. Today's postmodernist, New Age influenced, multiculturally sensitive, multimedia generation requires a more updated delivery system. Use of multimedia and visual illustrations might be considered, as well as checking the current meaning of words in our preaching vocabulary. Delivering the message of salvation through Jesus Christ to a generation that considers itself post-Christian is not easy, but that is precisely what we are called to do.

4. Personal Preparation: Preaching without power is not charismatic. Charismatic preaching involves the manifestation of the power of the Holy Spirit. The preparation of the preacher's heart and mind is essential in this regard. Pentecostal/charismatic preaching is confirmed by signs and wonders, the ultimate wonder being the conversion of a sinner. Since the preacher cannot manufacture signs and wonders, he must depend on God for them and prepare himself to move in the Spirit as He leads.

Maintaining personal integrity is another part of this preparation. Integrity provides credibility. Preachers are called to be credible witnesses. Lack of credibility undermines the vital message of the gospel. A faithful preacher must walk worthy of his calling. One walks worthy only when one walks in the Spirit!

31

INTEGRITY:
ADDRESSING THE SHORTAGE

A city bribes the Olympic Committee to host the winter games. Judges fix the gold medals way before the competitions. The leaders of the seventh-largest corporation in the country (Enron) exploit their employees and investors in scandalous trading practices, and each leader pleads the Fifth before congressional committees. Unfortunately, there was not one "Christian" businessman in that company to stand up and confess his mistakes or to say he abstained from the unethical practices.

These things happened some years ago, but it is undeniable that there is still a shortage of integrity in America. This should concern all citizens, especially those of us who value America's Christian heritage.

Psychologists and theologians agree that integrity is the highest level of human character. They agree that it is hard to sustain hope in a place without integrity. Erik Erikson, the famous social psychologist, theorized[16] that human life moves through eight stages. A person faces a crisis at each stage of life. He is healthy if he overcomes the crisis and suffers the consequences if he does not master the crisis. The first crisis in life, according to Erikson, is one of dealing with trust versus mistrust. The last one—the eighth—is the crisis of integrity versus despair.

Integrity is the secular word for hope. What Erikson was saying is that only those who have integrity can live and die in hope. Integrity allows one to speak the truth, and it makes one's words and deeds become congruent. It promotes love and unselfishness. Integrity makes people trustworthy.

According to the Word of God, all Christians should be living examples of integrity. Unfortunately, even among Christians integrity is not always found. What a tragedy! How wonderful it would have been to see one Christian man or woman stand up and own up to the truth at the Olympics or at Enron. How strange that the Christian community said almost nothing about these events. The newspaper editors and politicians have had more to say about integrity recently than the American preachers have! What would Jesus do?

The Bible says that our yes should be yes, and our no should be no (Matt. 5:37). The Pharisees were experts in external religion, and Jesus was not soft on them. We still face the same temptation to keep our faith external and our Christian distinctiveness superficial.

I am not calling Christians to go and turn over the tables of the money changers, but I do believe that the Lord is calling us to be people of integrity. He desires that we practice our faith

---

16 William Crain, *Theories of Development: Concepts and Applications* (Upper Saddle River, NJ: Pearson Education, Inc., 2011).

in all areas of our lives. It is time that we examine ourselves. We may not be bribing the Olympic Committee or robbing stock-holders and pensioners, but we also face many temptations to violate integrity.

People with integrity do not say one thing and do another, and they do not break their word. People with integrity do not assassinate the character of their peers or use anonymous letters to attack others. People with integrity do not cheat their employers. People with integrity do not cheat in voting.

We can model integrity before our neighbors and our children. We can demonstrate that Christ has truly transformed our lives. Our faith is not limited to the church buildings; we live out our faith daily in our communities. A life of faith is a life of integrity. Wouldn't it be wonderful if we were known as doers of the Word rather than hearers?

32

HOSPITAL CHAPLAINCY: PASTORING AN EVER-CHANGING SICK FLOCK

An increasing number of Pentecostal/charismatic ministers are entering the specialized field of hospital chaplaincy. This is indeed a welcome trend. The field of hospital chaplaincy has been dominated by clergy from mainline denominations for a variety of reasons, including lack of training and lack of emphasis in charismatic circles on this type of professional ministry. The entry of more Spirit-led clergy into this field will make a difference both in the nature of this special ministry and in the way it has been traditionally viewed by Pentecostals/charismatics.

Traditionally, hospital chaplains have been viewed more as counselors than as pastors. While chaplains do a lot of counseling, they are more than counselors. Chaplains are pastors who have been trained to skillfully and effectively pastor people in crisis.

Institutional chaplaincy may seem to be a modern trend, yet it is solidly rooted in Scripture. David ministered in Saul's courts; Nathan ministered in David's palace. Modern hospital chaplaincy is based on this rich tradition, and fulfills the expectation of the Lord Jesus expressed in Matthew 25:36: "I was sick, and ye visited me" (KJV).

The demands of pastoring and the busy daily schedule of modern pastors make it extremely difficult for them to offer all that the hospitalized among their flocks may need. Thus, the chaplains' ministry provides a great resource for pastors. A true alliance between local pastors and chaplains is not a luxury; it is a necessity.

It is widely accepted that every pastor needs someone to pastor him or her, and every chaplain needs a pastor too. A few chaplains are fortunate enough to have a chaplain in their own hospital who can pastor them, but in most cases one is not available. Even when one is, chaplains often need a pastor for their families.

A chaplain faces certain unique challenges. He serves a flock that is either sick or is dealing daily with the crises of illness. Another challenge is the attempt to build relationships in an ever-changing congregation made up of individuals from every conceivable spiritual background. Most of the chaplain's time is spent in crisis intervention.

Chaplaincy also presents tremendous opportunities. Many people are more open to a chaplain than to a pastor. A chaplain brings with him no demands for membership or conversion. He is not perceived to be there to "get them" while they are vulnerable (at least a few patients have misunderstood pastors in this area). This perception of the chaplain as nonthreatening opens wonderful opportunities to minister and to "win souls" (I use the term carefully).

There are church members in good standing who would not share at a deep level with their own pastor, yet they may feel free to talk with and receive counsel from another member of the clergy. There are even people who do not want their pastor to be informed of their hospitalization. This is not necessarily a reflection on the ability of the pastor, but is more a reflection of human nature. They may not wish to be seen at their worst by the pastor whose opinion of them seems so important.

Regardless of the chaplain's denominational affiliation, closer fellowship and communication between chaplains and local pastors is called for. A chaplain is more likely to send a new convert to the congregation of a pastor with whom he has himself established rapport.

It is essential that Spirit-filled ministers enter the specialized field of hospital ministry in greater numbers. In spite of all the skillful work that goes on, the ministry of the Holy Spirit is sadly lacking in the hospitals of America. This need is not met by occasional visits of Pentecostal pastors to see their own sick members. God is calling Spirit-filled men and women to commit their lives to a lifelong ministry on this American mission field.

For those who feel a burden, here is the required route to most chaplaincy positions: A candidate is required to have a master of divinity degree, and some field experience in institutional ministry is expected. Completion of the basic level of clinical pastoral education (CPE) is often required, with advanced training and pastoral experience considered a plus. Ordination and endorsement as a chaplain from a faith community is also required. Traditional Pentecostal denominations and organizations such as Chaplaincy for Full Gospel Churches can assist potential candidates in these matters. Institutions across the nation offer CPE training, and further information can be requested from: www.acpe.edu.

I would like to see the number of Spirit-filled chaplains significantly increase in clinical settings across the world.

33

CELEBRITY PASTORS
AND MERE SHEPHERDS

I had lunch with a local pastor yesterday in an American city. It was an enjoyable time of fellowship with a servant of God, sharing a simple meal of soup and sandwich. Our conversation included updates on our children and grandchildren and challenges and opportunities of ministry in the twenty-first century. All of a sudden, the pastor said, "I stopped burying other pastors' sheep."

"What do you mean?" I asked.

He said, "There are churches in this town with great reputation for having cutting-edge technology to reach the new generation where people do not know their pastors. When there is a death in the family, they don't know whom to call. I have been called so many times to bury their dead. I have done it for a while now, but I have decided to stop doing it so that I can pay more attention to my church members."

This conversation reflects the sad state of pastoral care in modern American churches. In a country where, according to AARP Magazine, 35% of people ages 45 and up are chronically lonely,[17] this is an indictment on the church. As a professor of pastoral care, I am extremely concerned about this situation.

Pastors of these high-tech churches say that they have mechanisms in place to meet the pastoral care needs of their members. This includes networks of small groups, with leaders who can minister to their group members. Thankfully, there are many churches that utilize small groups very effectively to address the pastoral care and discipleship needs of their members. However, this is not universally true. Many care groups are in effect didactic groups, and their leaders are not trained to care for their members.

Not long ago, I had a conversation with a young lady who left one of these high-tech churches. She left because her small-group leader began to date a member of the group, and the group's agenda changed weekly to meet their preferences and reflected the stage of their romantic relationship. The young woman called the church office to express her concern only to discover that the staff pastor in charge of groups was an untrained minister barely beyond his adolescence! She has since then found a healthier community of faith.

Are high-tech churches not effective? I am not saying that. They are serving a great purpose in this generation for the kingdom of God. They are great places to attract the unchurched and introduce them to Jesus Christ. They can also be a haven

---

17 Brad Edmondson, "All the Lonely People" [online]; available from https://www.aarp.org/personal-growth/transitions/info-09-2010/all-the-lonely-people.html.

for wounded Christians and people who are not ready for in-depth Christian fellowship. These churches are leading people to Christ who may not ever enter a traditional church. But these potentials do not excuse them for not offering effective pastoral care to those who consider them their church homes.

No, I am not saying that the senior pastor must do all the pastoral care in a congregation. Groups and group leaders can really be a blessing in this matter. However, the lead pastors bear the burden to make sure that true pastoral care actually takes place. This involves appointing well-trained pastors on the staff, training every group leader in pastoral-care skills, and having excellent communication systems within the churches to handle serious pastoral-care issues. This is actually doable. Bible colleges and seminaries can be rich resources for training not only the staff pastors, but also lay group leaders.

Meanwhile, if you happen to be a member of a not-so-mega church, with less-intense laser beams, where the pastor may not be an orator like your favorite online preacher, but is one who cares for your soul like a shepherd, instead of complaining about the weaker charisma or imperfect oration of that servant of God, simply get down on your knees and thank God for that person. God forbid, but if you happen to be in a real crisis, that shepherd will be there for you, following the Good Shepherd.

34

THE MINISTRY OF BLESSING

James (not his real name) was a fifty-five-year-old white male. He was an ordained minister of a major denomination, trying to finish his doctor of ministry thesis, and was having a tough time. He just could not write the main part of the thesis; it was more than a "writer's block." I listened to James as he tried to explain why he thought he could not produce the work. James still could hear his second grade teacher's voice in his head, speaking to him in a very angry voice: "You are stupid, James. You will amount to nothing!"

That episode had occurred forty-eight years in the past, but remained a loud echo in the adult James's mind, even after he had earned his bachelor's and master's degrees; and it still resounded as he was nearing completion of his doctorate. The truth is that James was a very intelligent person. He had been a successful pastor and leader, and a capable preacher of the Word. But deep in his heart, his wounds from the second grade remained, fighting against a greater achievement.

Our words have power, especially when we are in a position of authority, such as a teacher, pastor, or counselor. Our words impact ourselves and others in very profound ways.

As Christians, we believe that God made everything from nothing by the power of His Word. When He made us in His own image, one of the ways that we resembled Him was that we received verbal ability, not found in animals. Why should we be surprised, then, that in spite of the fall, our words carry power?

Please do not misunderstand my point. Some teachers have made Christians afraid to even express a need or a problem because of a fear that in so doing, they express a lack of faith. I am certainly not saying that our routine words are more powerful than God's Word. Yet our words do have power to impact both positively and negatively. We must choose our words with discernment, especially at crucial moments of someone's life.

Psychologists have already established the value of positive self-talk. People who speak positively to themselves live better lives. Negative self-talk has the opposite effect. Words can encourage as well as discourage, empower as well as dehumanize, bless as well as curse. Why not use our words to encourage, empower, and bless?

The power of blessing and cursing is made very clear in the Bible. There are plentiful illustrations of both. We read that God blessed Adam, Noah, and Abraham. Abraham in turn blessed his son Isaac. Isaac then blessed his son Jacob, albeit through a switch. Jacob's history shows that even a blessing received in deception carries its power. Later on, Jacob blessed Joseph, his other sons, and his grandsons.

The story of the people of Israel is the story of a blessed people. Even when they are disobedient, the blessings provide some protection from God's anger. Jacob's struggle with the Angel of the Lord by the river Jabbok and the blessing he received with "signs following" (limping) is described in detail in Genesis. The writer of Genesis wanted to make sure the world understood that the people of Israel represented the sons and daughters of a blessed man, a man blessed both by God and man. Although he deceived his father to gain his blessing, Jacob had to be brutally honest to be blessed by God.

The Bible records many other stories of blessings. Moses and Aaron as leaders gave their blessings to the people of Israel. The priests were instructed to bless the people with these words: "The LORD bless you and keep you; the LORD make his face shine on you and be gracious to you; the LORD turn his face toward you and give you peace" (Num. 6:24–26 NIV). Following the same tradition, David also blessed his people.

The history of blessings continues throughout the Bible. Although the story of the curse runs parallel to it, the blessing ultimately triumphs. God's blessings overcome the curse in all its forms.

The power of blessing is also very clearly illustrated in the New Testament. Jesus blessed the little children. According to Luke, the last act Jesus performed before His ascension was blessing: He lifted up His hands and blessed the disciples (Luke 24:50). Jesus came to bless the world. The blessing of the gospel came to us through those disciples. We are blessed and are called to bless others.

Unfortunately, we often do not bless others. We are eager to express our disapproval rather than our approval. We find ourselves cursing others instead of blessing them. It takes no more energy to bless than to curse; why, then, do we not bless? Why do we not verbally bless the ones we really want to see blessed?

This is a vital concept in parenting. All of us want our children blessed; yet how often do we bless them? Why do we let minor irritations prevent us from blessing our offspring? I believe we must look for opportunities to bless our children. Let them hear us blessing them. Let them remember our blessings. When they go out to face the world on their own, let them find strength and courage in the memory of the blessings we have pronounced over them. This thought alone must cause us to bless them, even if there were no other mystery in the power of blessing!

We must bless others also, including our family members and friends. Teachers must bless their students. Pastors, like the Old Testament priests, must bless their people. Supervisors should bless their associates, and why not? Current books on corporate leadership are addressing these issues of encouraging and uplifting employees. Blessing may be the most cost-effective employee benefit!

Suppose Pastor James's second grade teacher, instead of cursing him with a negative opinion forty-eight years ago, had said to the boy, "James, I bless you in the name of God. You are a blessed child. God will help you with your studies, and you will be a success. Remember, James: with God's help, you may even earn a doctorate someday!" Instead of cursing, that teacher could have planted a good seed of blessing in his life, using the same time and energy it took to curse him. Then he would not have been still haunted by those wounding words at age fifty-five. Instead, he would have remembered her with the fondest of thoughts and gratitude.

Thank God for the redeeming, healing power of the Holy Spirit. James did get his healing from the wounds of second grade, and he was able to complete his thesis and receive his doctorate. Today he is a powerful minister of the gospel; he is busy ministering to others who have also been wounded by careless words. With the help of the Holy Spirit, James finally found a way to break out of a forty-eight-year-old curse, and began to give blessing to others.

35

EMPOWERED TO
WALK, RUN, AND FLY

The book of Acts is one of my favorite books in the Bible. One reason is because the book unveils how people of different races, nationalities, and capacities entered the kingdom of God. For instance, the second chapter mentions 120 people who waited in the upper room in anticipation of the coming of the Holy Spirit. Most of these were Jewish. Chapter 3 introduces a handicapped man at the temple gate who wound up walking and leaping and praising God. Chapter 6 introduces Greek women who became church members. Other groups continue to show up in later chapters. An African is the central figure in chapter 8.

Acts 8 tells the story of Philip the witness. The Holy Spirit prompted him to go to Gaza. He got up and walked down the road that goes from Jerusalem to Gaza. On the road, Philip noticed an Ethiopian government official, a eunuch, traveling in a chariot. He was sitting in the back of the chariot and reading. The Spirit spoke to him again, "Go near and overtake this chariot"—not an easy assignment for a man on foot. Philip obeyed anyway and he "ran" (8:29–30).

As he approached the chariot, Philip could hear the Ethiopian reading from the book of Isaiah. He began a conversation with the man, which turned out to be a sermon. "He preached Jesus to him" (8:35). The Ethiopian believed what he heard and requested to be baptized in water. Philip baptized him in some kind of a roadside pond. "When they came up out of the water," something very interesting happened. The Bible says, "The Spirit of the Lord caught Philip away" and he was later found at Azotus (8:39–40).

I don't know what being caught away by the Spirit looks like. I can only imagine that it looked like flying.

Look at the journey of a witness. He began walking. Soon he was running. And when it was all over, he was flying! All led by the Spirit.

Being led by the Spirit is important for all disciples, as they are called to bear witness to Christ. I hope you will walk, run, and fly as a witness.

PART III

SPIRIT-EMPOWERED
DISCIPLESHIP

36

DEFINING
SPIRIT-EMPOWERED
DISCIPLESHIP

The Great Commission was and is a call to discipleship. Before His ascension, Jesus commissioned His followers to make disciples of all nations. It was a formidable task given to a group of unlikely candidates, but today, although the task still remains incomplete, there are billions of Christ's disciples around the world, testifying to the fact that the weak group in Jerusalem did something right. Acts 1 gives a clue to their success.

The mandate remains the same: the followers of Jesus are to make disciples of all ethnic groups (the Greek word translated as "nations" in Matt. 28:19 is *ethnos*). God's will is that the whole world be saved through faith in Jesus Christ and "Christ be formed in" each believer (Gal. 4:19 KJV). The ultimate purpose of this process is spiritual formation of every believer (Rom. 8:29).

Who is a disciple? The Bible defines the disciple of Jesus as a learner and follower. As a learner, one must develop character

(Gal. 5:22–23), convictions (Heb. 11:24–25), and skills (Mark 7:37). This learning process is expected to result in the development of a Christ-centered worldview and an eternal perspective on life.

A disciple must be a faithful follower of Jesus who must be willing to follow Jesus at any cost: "'Come, follow me,' Jesus said, 'and I will send you out to fish for people'" (Matt. 4:19 NIV). Luke reports: "'No one who puts a hand to the plow and looks back is fit for service in the kingdom of God'" (Luke 9:62 NIV). The disciple must follow the example of others who are faithful disciples: "Follow my example, as I follow the example of Christ," Paul said (1 Cor. 11:1 NIV).

There is an action dimension to discipleship. Theologians call this *praxis*. The disciples must put into practice what they learn from their Master. This may have to do with bearing witness to Christ in whatever means possible, such as preaching, teaching, and healing. "Whatever you have learned or received or heard from me, or seen in me—put it into practice. And the God of peace will be with you" (Phil. 4:9 NIV). In this sense, the disciple is an apprentice of Christ.

The Bible gives a clear description of the character requirements of a disciple. A disciple must abide in Christ (John 15:7), bear fruit (John 15:8), love Christ and others (Luke 14:26; John 13:34–35), and deny oneself (Luke 14:8–11). A true disciple is a cross-bearer: "Then he said to them all: 'Whoever wants to be my disciple must deny themselves and take up their cross daily and follow me'" (Luke 9:23 NIV).

How can anyone do this by one's own strength? This is where the clue from Acts makes sense. Jesus told His disciples, "But you will receive power when the Holy Spirit comes on you; and you will be my witnesses in Jerusalem, and in all Judea and Samaria, and to the ends of the earth" (Acts 1:8). It is the empowerment of the Holy Spirit that makes progressively following Christ possible. Spirit-empowered disciples make disciples. The same Spirit assists the disciple maker and the new disciple.

The weak band of locals in Jerusalem did not make a move until the Holy Spirit came upon them in the upper room (Acts 2:4). They obeyed Jesus and refused to leave Jerusalem without the required power.

The power did arrive. The disciples of Jesus did leave Jerusalem and make their way to the ends of the earth. This explains the existence of billions of disciples on the earth today. The task is still not complete. The assignment is not over. And the power has not been withdrawn. We must also receive that same power and be on our way, making disciples, transforming one *ethnos* at a time!

37

PENTECOSTAL SPIRITUALITY:
A CALL TO RETURN

Human beings are spiritual beings. There is a spiritual hunger in all humans that can be satisfied only by God. It is a vacuum in the soul of every person that can only be filled by the Creator. The vacuum in the heart of man longs for God.

Much of what we see as materialism and other excesses today is man's efforts to fill that gap with things other than God Himself. All religions try to address this issue in one way or another. The modern secular world tries to do this through habits, addictions, and New Age religions. But the truth is that genuine spiritual hunger will be satisfied only with a true encounter with the living God. And such an encounter is available only through Jesus Christ, the Son of the living God.

Generally speaking, there are two types of religions: one that has only the *appearance* of spiritual vitality, the other with true spirituality. In the words of the apostle Paul, there is a *form* of godliness without power on the one hand (2 Tim. 3:5 KJV), and *true* godliness with power on the other. It is easy for us to see powerless godliness in other religions, but unfortunately, many Christians' spirituality is only a form of godliness without the power thereof.

Pentecostal Spirituality

I believe that there is such a thing called Pentecostal spirituality. This is a spirituality that goes beyond having just the right doctrines. Of course, doctrines are absolutely important. Pentecostal doctrines of salvation, baptism, baptism in the Holy Spirit, divine healing, sanctification, and eschatology are very important. However, spirituality is more than a list of things we confess. It is more than the declaration of certain truths.

Stephen Land, a Pentecostal scholar in Cleveland, Tennessee, says that Pentecostal spirituality has beliefs, practice, and affections.[18] That is, Pentecostal spirituality presupposes the right beliefs and expects the right practices, but it also involves the right affections.

Land says that Pentecostal spirituality is Christocentric, meaning Christ is the center of this spirituality. To him, this Christ-centered spirituality is based on a fivefold gospel of salvation, sanctification, healing, baptism in the Holy Spirit, and the Second Coming.[19] For Pentecostals, salvation is more than conversion. It is a journey, a pilgrimage. Pentecostals are pilgrims. According to Land, Pentecostals practice their faith in light of the

---

18 Stephen Jack Land, *Pentecostal Spirituality: A Passion for the Kingdom* (Cleveland TN, CPT Press, 2010), 31.
19 Land, 12.

in-breaking of the kingdom of God,[20] which breaks into our lives through spiritual worship, walking in the Spirit, and witnessing.

In other words, Pentecostal spirituality involves the right beliefs (orthodoxy) and the right practices (orthopraxy). These are integrated in the right affections (orthopathy). What are these deep affections? According to Land, they are gratitude, compassion, courage,[21] and the kingdom of God.[22] The kingdom of God is the overarching affection. That is, the awareness of the kingdom of God rules all else.

Stephen Land is describing true Pentecostal spirituality, in which many of us were raised. Many of us are eyewitnesses of a group of ordinary people who lived this life in its spiritual fullness. We were forever impacted by them.

Current Status

Although there are exceptions, I must sadly state that genuine Pentecostal spirituality is on the decline today. Although Pentecostal doctrines are under attack and behaviors need improvement, the main backsliding has been in the area of affections. Here is my observation: if gratitude, compassion, courage, and the kingdom of God used to be our affections, today the following "affections" seem to be more highly regarded: entitlement, competition, security, and personal kingdom—entitlement instead of gratitude, competition instead of compassion, security instead of courage, and personal kingdom instead of the kingdom of God.

---

20 Land. See "Pentecostal Presence: The Inbreaking of the Spirit in the Last Days" in chap. 2 (pp. 51–62).
21 Land, 134–35.
22 Land. See "Pentecostal Affections: Embodying and Longing for the Kingdom" in chap. 3 (pp. 120–61).

Gratitude versus Entitlement

Once Pentecostals gathered together to express their profound gratitude to God for their salvation and all the provisions He had given to a marginalized people. They sang and testified. They fasted and prayed. They gathered together as often as possible. Distance was not a problem. Lack of easy transportation was not an issue. They were simply grateful. It appears that gratitude has been replaced by a sense of entitlement. It is the mind-set of the prodigal son before he left home. The father owes the son. He is entitled to his inheritance. He does not have to be grateful. So, worship has to be pumped up now. Praise has to be squeezed out. Singing at conventions and conferences has been delegated to highly paid music groups. They are no longer worship leaders. They do the worship for us!

Compassion versus Competition

Competition has replaced compassion. Evangelism used to be based on love for the lost. Then, we were saved to serve. Now it is a matter of who is in charge. We want to be larger and louder than the other group. We are willing to duplicate any ineffective efforts at a higher cost just to keep up with the Joneses. It is all about us. We have conferences without purpose and gatherings without cause.

Courage versus Security

Pentecostal courage has become another casualty. The pioneering Pentecostals had courage to witness to a hostile culture. They were deprived and abused, but they had the courage to stand up for what they believed. No, it was not about politics and elections. It was not a matter of slogans. It was about having

142

convictions and the guts to stand up for them. Their personal security was not their main concern.

God's Kingdom versus Personal Kingdoms

In many circles, ministry now has become building personal kingdoms. Nothing much is said about the kingdom of God. It is about "my ministry," not "His ministry." Self-promotion is our mode of operation. Gospel stardom is our goal. Leaders are everywhere; servants are few. Ministries are everywhere; ministers are few. Crusades are everywhere; converts are few. Dignitaries are everywhere; disciples are few!

A Call

This is the fact: Our backsliding is not subtle. Our Pentecostal affections are not only being neutralized; they are being reversed. This must stop. I believe that God is calling us back. He is calling us to repentance. God is calling us to true Pentecostal spirituality of beliefs, practice, and sacred affections—gratitude, compassion, courage, and the kingdom of God. We must heed His call—for our own sake and for the sake of the world.

38

A BIBLICAL VIEW OF IDENTITY
FOR CHRISTIAN YOUTH

Erik Erikson, the noted psychoanalyst, has done significant research in the area of youth and identity. After studying all the stages of human life and the unique problems of each stage, Erikson claims that the most significant issue for young people is the question of identity. Experts say that the question of identity is even more crucial for first-generation Americans, such as children of immigrants.

It is true that many are seeking to find themselves. It is very important to know who one is. Unfortunately, various cults and groups that lead people into serious error are taking advantage of this natural searching. It is pathetic to see millions innocently turning toward cults, non-Christian meditations, and mantras of the Eastern religions to find their identity.

Formation of self-identity is an essential part of every human's development. Everyone has a deep need to know "who he is." It is God's will for us to know who we are, and He has given us insights regarding this matter in the Bible:

Christian: A Child of God

A Christian is one who has been born again into a new identity, which he must discover. He has been adopted into God's family. He is an heir of the Father and joint-heir with Jesus Christ. He has the privilege of calling the almighty God by the familiar term *Abba* (Father).

"The Spirit itself beareth witness with our spirit, that we are the children of God: And if children, then heirs; heirs of God, and joint-heirs with Christ" (Rom. 8:16–17 KJV). "But as many as received him, to them gave he power to become the sons of God, even to them that believe on his name" (John 1:12 KJV). "Beloved, now are we the sons of God" (1 John 3:2 KJV).

What a privilege it is to know that, as Christians, we belong to the greatest family on earth. May this knowledge be always upon your mind and your spirit. May you always be able to say, "I am a child of God!"

Christian: A Sinner Saved

"Please be patient; God is not finished with me yet," reads a popular bumper sticker. Another says, "Christians aren't perfect, just forgiven." These express two great truths. A Christian must never assume that he is somehow superior to his fellow human beings. He is, of course, a child of God, and yet remains a sinner saved by the grace of God, a sinner forgiven. The apostle Paul was always conscious of his status as a saved sinner. He wrote to Timothy: "This is a faithful saying, and worthy of all acceptation, that Christ Jesus came into the world to save sinners, of whom I am chief. Howbeit . . . I obtained mercy" (1 Tim. 1:15–16 KJV).

Paul also reminded the Christians at Ephesus about their status as saved sinners: "For by grace are ye saved through faith; and that not of yourselves: it is the gift of God" (Eph. 2:8 KJV). The mystery of the gospel is that we are forgiven sinners who are called to become saints, "set-apart ones." We are to live "as becometh saints" (Eph. 5:3 KJV).

Christian: A Citizen of Heaven

A person born in a particular country becomes a citizen of that country. Since a Christian is born into the kingdom of heaven, this makes him or her a citizen of that kingdom. Some countries used to sell citizenship; one had to pay a large amount of money to purchase citizenship. We could never afford to pay the cost for our heavenly citizenship; Jesus paid the price for our citizenship at Calvary. He gives this purchased citizenship free of charge; it is His absolutely free gift to us.

Even though he was proud to be a citizen of the great Roman Empire, Paul was not ashamed to proclaim that "our citizenship is in heaven" (Phil. 3:20). "Now therefore ye are no more strangers and foreigners, but fellowcitizens with the saints, and of the household of God" (Eph. 2:19 KJV). Our new citizenship in heaven makes us aliens on the earth. Our life and manners must reflect our foreign citizenship. Our conversation should reflect a holy accent in our language.

The early church fathers tell us that the Old Testament saints anticipated this "foreign" citizenship. "By faith he [Abraham] sojourned in the land of promise, as in a strange country, dwelling in tabernacles with Isaac and Jacob . . . for he looked for a city which hath foundations, whose builder and maker is God" (Heb. 11:9–10 KJV). "These all died in faith, not having received the promises, but having seen them afar off, and were persuaded of them, and embraced them, and confessed that they were strangers and pilgrims on the earth. . . . They desire a better country, that is, an heavenly" (Heb. 11:13, 16 KJV).

Christian: A Disciple and a Servant

We are disciples of Christ. We are not to be just one of the multitude that comes to see the miracles; we are called to stay with the Master even after the multitude leaves. We are His servants. We have not chosen Him; He has chosen us. We are not worthy; He is. It is our simple privilege to serve Him. We love Him because He first loved us. Jesus said, "If any man serve me, let him follow me; and where I am, there shall also my servant be. If any man serve me, him will my father honour" (John 12:26 KJV).

Paul wrote to the Colossians about the behavior expected of a Christian: "And whatsoever ye do, do it heartily, as unto the Lord, and not unto men; knowing that of the Lord ye shall receive the reward of the inheritance: for ye serve the Lord Christ" (Col. 3:23–24 KJV).

As previously stated, various cults and groups that lead people into serious error take advantage of the natural search of young people for identity. Churches and ministries must provide opportunities for young people to discover their true identities in Christ. Youth pastors should make this concern a priority as they plan and design ministry activities.

39

ADDRESSING
THE DISCIPLESHIP CHALLENGE

In this era of "praise and worship," "fire conferences," and "mega" everything, the modern church is suffering from a real shortage of Christian discipleship. This seems especially true within fellowships where, generally speaking, no teaching is deemed necessary beyond children's Sunday school. How should this issue be addressed?

The American situation can shed some light on this matter. For instance, 77 percent of Americans identify themselves as Christian. Forty-four percent say they belong to a Christian congregation, but only 20 percent actually show up to worship weekly.[23] What is the problem? An increasing number of Chris-

---

23 Frank Newport, "In U.S., 77% Identify as Christian," Gallup News, December 24, 2012, http://news.gallup.com/poll/159548/identify-christian. aspx; Ed Stetzer, "Too Many So-Called Christians Merely Giving Lip Service to Jesus," Charisma News, March 28, 2014, https://www.charismanews. com/opinion/43298-christian-it-s-more-than-just-a-label; Kelly Shattuck, "7 Startling Facts: An Up Close Look at Church Attendance in America,"

tians are cultural Christians, just as many Hindus are cultural Hindus in India. There seem to be three groups of Christians: (1) cultural Christians, (2) congregational Christians, and (3) true disciples of Christ. It appears that crusades that ask people to "make a decision" for Christ are not necessarily producing "converts" and "disciples."

There are Christians who affirm the Christian confession, but do not live what they confess. They will claim that they "believe," but do not practice what they believe. They may belong to a church, but do not feel the obligation to support the church. These are spectator Christians, "sloganized" constituents, not participating disciples.

Cultural Christianity or nominal Pentecostalism will not produce true followers of Christ. God wants to develop Christ's disciples. He is looking for men and women who have counted the cost of following Christ in their generation. He is looking for people who do not mind being different in this conforming world. He wants to make them citizens of heaven and participants in the kingdom of God.

Studies have shown that discipleship has to be intentional. Disciples are not made accidentally. The church must make disciple making a priority—not just crowd gathering. The Word of God must be central to the task of disciple making. God's word is a disciple's rule book for faith and practice. A community of faith is needed to develop disciples. This has to be much smaller than mega. It takes a small group to train disciples. Disciples are formed and shaped in the community of faith. This can certainly

---

Church Leaders, December 14, 2017, https://churchleaders.com/pastors/pastor-articles/139575-7-startling-facts-an-up-close-look-at-church-attendance-in-america.html.

happen within a megachurch or large ministry, but the actual formational work happens in a smaller group of committed followers of Jesus who are guided by godly mentors.

Every church needs a plan to develop disciples. It takes more than love and support. It takes a commitment to provide the teaching and the relationships to make it happen. The Lord's command is not "Gather a crowd," but "Make disciples" (Matt. 28:19)!

40

BEING A HOPE BEARER

The last days of the year 2017 witnessed major turmoil all around the world. Syria was on fire. Superpowers were in conflict. Terrorism was on the increase in many parts of the world. International tensions were increasing, especially in Asia and Europe.

Today, there is trouble in the South China Sea waters. Turkey is under severe tension. Trade wars are predicted as globalization is under serious scrutiny. Nationalism is on the rise in Europe and America. Political alignments are unraveling across the globe.

Populations in many nations are proving that they have lost faith in their own leaders and national institutions. Brexit, Great Britain's exit from the European Union, surprised the pundits and the elites. The election of Mr. Donald Trump as president of the United States was seen as a surprise and has been watched with curiosity around the world even as the US stock market has boomed since his election.

Intranational problems also abound globally. The currency problem in India and the immigration issues in America are examples of this, with potentially far reaching consequences.

There are people who see parallels between 2017–18 and the beginning decades of the twentieth century, particularly before the First World War. They point out that the previous century began with major problems and ended up with the Great War, and they call for prayer for things to calm down soon.

Five causes of World War I have been identified: (1) issues related to mutual defense alliances, (2) imperialism, (3) military buildup, (4) nationalism, and (5) assassinations.[24] These look frighteningly familiar in today's world. How should Spirit-filled Christians conduct themselves in this context?

Unfortunately, the Spirit-filled division of the Christian family has a history of histrionics when it comes to world events. It has been noticed that some among us get hyperactive in predicting the worst possible scenarios during times like this. I have seen wild interpretations of Bible passages used by some to justify their dreadful predictions of doom and gloom.

I believe there is a better way. I also believe that frightening is not the best way to get people into the kingdom of God or to help believers live holy lives. Love works much better.

At the root of a lot of problems in the world today is hopelessness. Hopeless people do terrible things. Bullets alone will not stop them or change them. Hope will. The good news of Jesus Christ will.

Christians are people of hope. Spirit-filled Christians must be the best specimen of hope-filled Christians. While biblical

---

24 Kelly, Martin. "5 Key Causes of World War I." ThoughtCo., updated January 30, 2018, https://thoughtco.com/causes-that-led-to-world-war-i-105515.

prophesies will definitely come to pass, we should not use them to frighten people or routinely predict doom. All biblical prophesies are not about doom and gloom.

Our God is a God of hope. We must demonstrate real hope in this hopeless world. This is not a call to denial, as indeed there are serious problems in the world. Christ is the only answer to these problems. The followers of Jesus will find real peace and experience God's care and protection even during the worst of times. And Jesus will definitely come again.

Until then, we must bear witness to the gospel of Jesus Christ. We are people who know that weeping may last through the night, but joy will come in the morning (Ps. 30:5). We know that God can change our sorrow to joy, our darkness to light, and our weeping to laughter. We know that He will wipe away all our tears one day.

Until then, let us bear witness to the hope we have in Jesus Christ. Let us show the world how to live as followers of the Prince of Peace. Let us demonstrate hope-filled lives and love people into the kingdom of God. Let us be hope bearers.

We should be able to enter the future with hope as we trust the presence, power, and promises of our God. This is definitely possible. Listen to the apostle Paul: "Christ in you, the hope of glory" (Col. 1:27).

41

DEALING WITH TEMPTATIONS

God's people have an enemy. He uses temptations to cause backsliding because his desire is to steal, kill, and destroy. All Christians are tempted. In fact, Jesus our Lord Himself was tempted by the devil. Being tempted is not a sin. Yielding to temptation is.

The devil normally strikes believers at their weakest spots. For instance, Jesus had been fasting for forty days and nights. He was physically weak and hungry. The devil approached him with the issue of bread at such a time.

We can learn much from the temptation of Jesus. First, notice that He was led into the desert by the Holy Spirit to be tempted (Matt. 4:1). The Spirit knew that we would need to learn from Jesus how to overcome temptations.

Jesus was tempted in the areas of appetite, power, and pride. He was tempted with the bread question first (v. 3). This was followed by the temptation regarding a demonstration of power. He was asked to jump off the pinnacle of the temple (vv.

5–6). Then came the final temptation as a matter of idolatry. The devil asked Jesus to worship him. In return he would give Him the whole world (vv. 8–9)! The Son of the living God was being offered all the kingdoms of this world as if they were not already His.

The devil tempts the followers of Jesus the same way. They are tempted regarding the lust of the flesh, the lust of the eyes, and the pride of life (1 John 2:16).

The temptation of Jesus demonstrates how we can overcome temptations. The main weapon is the sword of the Spirit, which is the Word of God (Eph. 6:17). Jesus kept on quoting the Word of God. "It is written . . . ," Jesus said in response to each temptation (Matt. 4:4, 6, 7, 10).

We not only have the written word. We also have the living Word—Jesus—dwelling in us. Jesus lives in us through the Holy Spirit. We need to be aware that "greater is he that is in [us], than he that is in the world" (1 John 4:4 KJV).

We should grieve whenever a believer falls. Fallen Christian leaders are monuments of the devil's strategy to defeat God's servants. We should pray for one another and help each other in Christian walk.

42

SAYING THANK YOU
AFTER FOUR DECADES

I just received a letter from a New Yorker named Cathy (not her real name) whom I have met only once, in the sky, nearly four decades ago!

September 8, 1972! The day I arrived in the United States! With a college degree and very little travel experience, I was on my way to attend Yale University Divinity School in New Haven, Connecticut. With big dreams and bigger apprehensions, I had begun my journey from Cochin airport in southwestern India on September 7.

After a night in Bombay and a couple of stops in the Middle East, I arrived in London. I left London on a British Airways (then known as BOAC) flight to New York. Seated next to me on that flight were two black females—one young woman and the other who could have been her mother.

I had sent a letter to a relative in New York before I left India, informing him of my arrival, but was not sure that he received my message. The thought of arriving in Kennedy Airport without anyone meeting me there was frightening to me. I had the ticket to continue my journey from New York to the tiny airport in New Haven, but had no idea how to make the transfer in New York. My mind was filled with petrifying thoughts about being stranded in New York with only eight dollars in my pocket, the maximum amount of cash India would let anyone take out then!

My fear must have been visible. The women sitting next to me inquired about my situation. I told them my dilemma. They told me that they were New Yorkers, and that if I needed any help at JFK, they would assist me. Their kind words gave me much comfort. As we were landing in New York, they took the little notebook I had in my hand and wrote their addresses and phone numbers in it and said, "Not only today, but as long as you are in the United States, if you run into any need, don't hesitate to call us. We will help you."

As we came out of immigration at JFK airport, I was relieved to find my relative waiting for me with several friends of his. The ladies said good-bye, and I have never seen them since.

Recently I came across that old notebook. After all these years, I noticed the addresses and phone numbers written in unfamiliar handwritings. I realized that I never called them for any help. I also realized that I had never said thank you to them for their kindness.

Where would you find them after all these years? Who knows what these women's names might be now? I tried to forget the whole thing, but a need to say thank you lingered.

My wife joined me in my search for these women from my past. The phone numbers they supplied proved useless. So, we decided to use the internet, which yielded one of the two names and two addresses. We had no idea if we had the right person, but I decided to write a letter of self-introduction and gratitude and mailed it to both addresses.

The letter I sent to Florida came back with the words "Addressee Unknown"! The response from New York came in a big envelope with Cathy's story.

Cathy was the younger of the two women I had met in the sky. Her senior companion was her friend and mentor. They were in London, visiting Cathy's relatives there, and were on their way back on that flight in 1972. Her mentor had died in 1990.

Cathy never married, so her name never changed. She took care of her disabled parents until they passed away. Her mother had died in 2003. She lost her father in 2006. Soon after, she was diagnosed with cancer, but is in remission now. Still she finds time to help the needy in her community.

It appears that my thank-you note lifted up Cathy's spirit. I don't know if she ever wondered what happened to the scared young man from India. But I am well aware of the blessings I have received in America. And of my indebtedness to many: Parents. Teachers. Spouse. Friends. Colleagues. Mrs. Livingstone, whom I met in a church foyer on my first Sunday in America, who gave me an unforgettable gift—two one-dollar bills from her Social Security income! And Cathy, whose kind words calmed my fears so long ago and welcomed me to America.

43

MICHAEL JACKSON AND
A LOST GENERATION

I was having lunch with some colleagues when the topic of singer Michael Jackson's death came up. This was the day before his "billion-people-watching" memorial service held at the Staples Center in Los Angeles, California. The professors were surprised at the magnitude of the attention and honor given to the entertainer. They noted that the predicted size of the crowd watching worldwide was unprecedented, larger than the funerals of Princess Diana and Mother Teresa.

Regardless of one's musical taste, one must admit that Mr. Jackson was a gifted musician and performer who came from a family of gifted and talented entertainers. His music influenced a whole generation globally. I have seen his "moves" performed by kids in faraway India!

I am told that Jackson was a notable philanthropist, but he never claimed to be a religious personality. He seemed to be a man in pain all the time, and it appears from the way he died that he was in pain physically and emotionally at the end. I certainly felt bad for his loved ones.

The fact remains that he was called "the King," greater than the other King, in Memphis—Elvis. Based on television news, in one of the tributes given to Jackson, Madonna, another mega entertainer, screamed, "Long live the King!"

Artists have a way of endearing themselves to their fans. All of us have our favorite singers, speakers, or artists. However, what creates a phenomenon such as Jackson? It is more than appreciation of his artistic gifts. There is something more going on in our culture of entertainment.

I got a clue to Mr. Jackson's appeal after I saw the *Today* show on NBC the day of the memorial service. The news show featured comments by Al Sharpton, the clergyman-politician from New York, and other well-known personalities, and interviews with Jackson fans who had come to Los Angeles without tickets to attend the memorial service, and in some cases without any money. I was watching the show while not enjoying the morning walk on my treadmill. I was shocked to hear a young woman say of Michael Jackson, "For our generation, he was the closest we got to God!" I could not believe what I'd just heard. I got off the treadmill and pondered her words.

Obviously, Michael Jackson represented God to this young lady, and to a multitude of other people. That is what the bereaved crowd was all about.

Indeed, we have a new generation. This hurting, internet-connected-but-alienated generation is desperately looking for God in its own ways. To many who were seeking God through art forms, Michael Jackson was a kind of incarnation.

We have a generation that worships heroes. Their heroes are not preachers, teachers, social workers, or librarians. They are performers and entertainers regardless of their values or lifestyles, who can lift them out of their pain at least momentarily.

Hinduism claims multiple incarnations. The Bible says that the Word became flesh and dwelt among us. God in Jesus "moved into the neighborhood," says the *Message* version of the Bible (John 1:14 MSG). According to Christian faith, Jesus Christ was the once-and-for-all incarnation of God. All are called to follow Him, to be like Him. Followers of Jesus are expected to live truly incarnational lives, revealing the love of God through their lives and lifestyles. Unfortunately, in many circles, Christians are not seen today as hope bearers.

Obviously, Jackson's music lifted the interviewee and her peers to some heights where their pain was less and hopelessness was bearable. To her, that is how close she had gotten to God.

This must be a challenge to all of us. There is a lost and hurting world that is looking for those who care, those who can lift it to a place of faith, hope, and lack of pain. We are called to be that people who can touch the hurting and lead them to the real God. Only in Him can one find lasting peace and joy. We must live up to this calling and reveal the eternal God to a hurting generation. This is what I have learned as I witnessed through television the largest memorial service ever held.

44

GOD AS FATHER, MOTHER, AND SHEPHERD

Human beings' understanding of God is limited. It is limited because we know God only as much as He has chosen to reveal Himself to us, and because what He has revealed already is too great for us to fully grasp. Science, for instance, is struggling to comprehend even a fraction of what has been revealed of God in nature.

Jesus Christ is the ultimate revelation of God. He revealed God for our fullest comprehension. Jesus called God His Father and taught us to call Him our Father. We naturally believe that God is our heavenly Father; this is absolutely proper.

The church throughout the ages has emphasized the Fatherhood of God, which some believe has limited the world's perception of God to that one role. Some feminists were offended by this history, claiming that it is the consequence of males being the sole authority figures in the church, resulting in the neglect of the contributions and needs of women. Some feminists have even gone to the extent of showing God as mother only, praying "Our mother who art in heaven . . ."! Others have proceeded to call God "Sophia—the goddess of wisdom." This has not been helpful.

The truth is that the Bible gives a variety of images of our God and Maker. These images have all been inspired by the Holy Spirit, and they all should be taken seriously.

The strongest image of God in the Bible is that of a Father (Matt. 6:9). God is our Everlasting Father (Isa. 9:6). Jesus taught us to call God "Abba, Father" (Mark 14:36). One description of God in the Psalms states, "As a father has compassion on his children, so the LORD has compassion on those who fear him" (103:13 NIV). What a privilege it is to call God our Father!

Unfortunately, we live in a world where many people have had negative experiences with their fathers. One hears terrible stories every day about abusive fathers, who inflict pain and suffering on their children. This is a major problem in the West due to the rampant rate of divorce and remarriage. I have heard of fathers burning their infants with their lighted cigarettes or making their children stand in very hot bath water as punishment for crying. Victims of "fatherly" abuse do not generally establish a positive image of God in their minds when God is described to them only as Father. They may associate God with their cruel earthly fathers and totally misunderstand God's eternal love that passes all understanding. It is possible that the Word of God also uses the image of God as mother for the sake of these and other wounded people.

"As a mother comforts her child, so will I comfort you," promises the Lord (Isa. 66:13 NIV). This image of God as a loving, comforting mother in the Word, is reinforced by several examples from nature. "Jerusalem, Jerusalem, you who kill the prophets and stone those sent to you, how often I have longed to gather your children together, as a hen gathers her chicks under her wings, but you were not willing" (Matt. 23:37 NIV). This verse illustrates that God protects His children like a mother hen that will go to any extreme to guard her chicks, sometimes at great peril to her own self.

A similar example is given in Deuteronomy 32:11: "Like an eagle that stirs up its nest and hovers over its young, that spreads its wings to catch them and carries them aloft." According to this passage, God cares about us and wants to teach us like a parent. As the parent eagle teaches its young to fly by making the nest uncomfortable, so also God does whatever it takes to enable us to fly above the problems of earthly life. We should not doubt God during temporary periods of discomfort or assume that all of these come from the devil. In God we have a loving parent, whose ultimate will is our growth and well-being. We can trust this God. That is my perception of the message of this image.

Another powerful image of God in the Word is that of a Shepherd. David declared, "The LORD is my shepherd; I shall not want (Ps. 23:1)." "I myself will tend my sheep," God said through Ezekiel (Ezek. 34:15 NIV). Jesus revealed the nature of the Good Shepherd when He said, "I am the good shepherd. The good shepherd lays down his life for the sheep" (John 10:11 NIV). God's love is unconditional and self-sacrificing.

The Bible reveals God's nature and character in multiple ways. For example, the various images presented in the Bible reveal different aspects of God's love for us. All of these images are relevant. Although one image may mean more to an individual, for personal reasons, than others do, all images continue to have their place and purpose. The Bible is God's message, and it must relate to all tribes, nations, and time periods. One should not insist that one's favorite image is the only image. God relates to us in personal and corporate ways; He knows what language or image communicates clearly to each individual. To one, He says, "I love you like a father"; to another, the same message is communicated when He says, "I love you like a mother" or "I will care for you like a shepherd." God knows how to get His message through to each one of us. Who are we to question His wisdom?

45

IS GOD CALLING YOU?

The Word of God tells us of people whom God called for specific purposes. The Old Testament speaks of Abraham, Moses, Samuel, Elijah, and others. The New Testament points out Andrew, Peter, and Paul, whom Jesus called. Church history tells us about others, like Augustine and Luther, who were also called by God.

There was a time when mothers used to pray for God to call their children to His work. We read about people such as the mother of John Wesley in this regard. Similar stories used to be heard among the earlier Pentecostals. For example, Oral Roberts's mother dedicated him for ministry when he was in her womb.

Unfortunately, we seldom hear such stories today, particularly in America. Young people tell me that their parents tell them to go into this or that profession. They are seldom asked to consider going into the ministry. There is nothing wrong with parents guiding their children into good professional fields. Yet, on the other hand, full-time ministry must not be eliminated from consideration.

Please don't misunderstand me. Not everyone is called to full-time Christian service, and not everyone needs to attend Bible college or seminary. You can serve humanity as a doctor, a dentist, or a pharmacist. God wants His people in all professions. However, there are some among us who must commit their lives to full-time ministry as pastors, teachers, missionaries, or evangelists. These are special offices and functions of ministry. Certain people are called to these specific ministries. All Christians—young and old—must be aware of this fact.

God's call has private and public aspects. We may sense the call of God as a private matter. Often that sense of call is confirmed by other Christians as one's gifts become more and more apparent. Parents and pastors are to be part of this confirmation process. That is why all parents should be seeking the Lord to discern God's purposes for their children.

Ministry is not a lucrative field. As adults who understand the economic realities of life, we do not want our children to experience the kind of economic hardships we have experienced or witnessed. That is why we want our kids to enter well-paying professions. This is understandable, but it is not a good enough reason to stand in God's way.

There is another possibility in ministry: entering a profession, like Paul the "tentmaker" (Acts 18:3 NIV), to support oneself in a ministry outside that profession. Those who choose this path must prepare for a profession *and* ministry. Missionaries who teach English as a foreign language in the developing world belong to this group.

Everyone entering full-time Christian service must take some time to prepare for it. Untrained ministers make many unnecessary mistakes and cause much damage to the kingdom of God. The idea that anyone with a pulse can offer high-quality ministry is not biblical or practical. Doctors are trained. Dentists are trained. Pharmacists are trained. Ministers MUST also be trained.

Is God calling you to some kind of Christian service? If you are planning to engage in any type of ministry, lay or ordained, please set aside some time for training. Full-timers and tentmakers must seek high-level training in Bible colleges and/or seminaries.

If you do not sense the call of God at this time, relax and pursue the vocation of your choice and be the best disciple of Jesus you can be in it. But if you do sense a tug on your heart, please talk to someone—your parents, pastors, or others—about what you are sensing in your spirit. If what you are sensing is real, your gifts will reveal themselves and your call will be confirmed by others. Be willing to take one step at a time by faith. There is abundant joy in doing God's will. May it be yours!

46

CHANGING THE WORLD —ONE PERSON AT A TIME

I know a young Spirit-filled woman who recently graduated from a public high school. Soon after the day she wore her cap and gown and said good-bye to her friends, she received a letter from a classmate who said her life had been touched by this Pentecostal young lady by something she had done several years before. Actually, it was by something she had not done. According to the letter, this classmate had noticed that long ago, in a middle school class, when all the students were cheating on a mathematics test, this young lady had refused to join her classmates. The writer had noticed her refusal to cheat, but had said nothing about it to her all these years. Now she was writing to acknowledge that the Pentecostal's conduct that day had impacted her life in a positive way.

I was speaking with another young Christian recently. She is a high school senior who decided to spend her summer vacation doing volunteer work at a nursery school for low-income people. She went to the nursery faithfully every day and cared for about a dozen four-year-olds. Many of these kids came from broken homes. Some displayed significant evidence of family problems and emotional abuse.

One particular little boy especially caught her attention. This boy—let's call him Billy—did not say a word to anyone. He was very insecure and cried constantly. He had all the symptoms of an emotionally needy child. This young lady tried to reach out to him. Every day she tried to show him that she cared about him, but there was no response.

Finally, the summer came to an end and she had to leave the volunteer work. Her last day at the nursery, the high school student took some cookies for everyone in her class. She said good-bye to each child. Finally, she came to Billy, gave him a cookie, and told him that she would be leaving to go back to school. She did not expect Billy to respond because he usually did not. But this day was different. Billy grabbed the cookie, looked up, and said, "Thank you!" Obviously, little Billy was touched by her life, and he responded!

Jesus told us, His disciples, to go into all the world. He told us that we are the light of the world. He taught us that we are the salt of the earth. The challenge is to find ways to let our light shine. The difficult task is to let our salt bring taste to others. How does one live as light and salt in today's world?

Many Christians want to change the whole world. They have great plans and mega ideas to reach the world, but no workable steps to get there. The fact is that there is a powerful way to change the world; that is to change it one person at a time. We cannot change people's hearts by force, but we can impact their lives by our lifestyle. A life touched by a true Christian's life is more apt to receive Christ.

Preaching has its place. Crusades are important. But the most important thing individual Christians can do is to live out their faith daily before the world. People are watching us. They want to know whether there is any truth to our claims of conversion and Christian commitment. We must remember that our actions speak louder than words. Godly actions can bring healing and wholeness to others.

Our actions have the power to bring healing or hurt. Our lifestyle has the power to change lives. Being the light and salt means living out our Christian convictions in a humble way. Positively impacting the people in our sphere of influence is the best way to lead the world to a full knowledge of Christ. God wants us to change our world. By the power of the Holy Spirit, we can fulfill this divine expectation. However, an excellent way to change our world is to change it one person at a time.

47

IMMIGRANTS AND DISCIPLESHIP

Have you ever read the Bible as a book about immigration? Not long ago, I came to the realization that the Bible has much to say about immigrants and their lives.

From the story of Abraham in Genesis, through the history of the exodus from Egypt, and all the way to the book of Revelation, where we are all on our way to the celestial city, the Bible depicts people in transit. Maybe it is because I am an immigrant that I see Jacob, Isaac, Joseph, Moses, Joshua, Caleb, Naomi, Ruth, Elijah, and Daniel and all his friends as immigrants. This discovery has made reading the Bible a fascinating experience for me.

I like to read about immigrants and their lives because they have exciting lives of challenges and opportunities, problems and possibilities, adjustments and maladjustments, hope and despair, and exploitation and excellence. Look, for example, at the life of Abraham. He leaves for a country he knows nothing about, but has the courage to take off. The Bible calls his courage *faith*. Think of Ruth. She decides to journey with her mother-in-law to her former land with no sponsors, no guides, and no guarantees. "Your people shall be my people," she swears about a people she has never met (Ruth 1:16)!

Think of Joseph. The young man who makes his way through the pit to Potiphar's house, to the prison, and eventually to the prime minister's office! What a journey! Think of Daniel—a man who becomes an immigrant against his own will. He was a captive taken to Babylon. He did not enjoy a lot of freedom, but he received the best education available in that land and made it to the top in Babylon by being faithful to his God. He overcame temptations and challenges. He kept his integrity and hope. He became a solution to many of the problems of the new land.

The biblical immigrants found many problems—even in the Promised Land. To overcome them, they had to learn to trust God.

I have observed several things about immigrants of all ages through my reading of the Bible as a book about immigrants. I will mention the top three observations here and then briefly explain them. First, God is in charge of immigration, not anyone else. Second, God takes care of immigrants. Third, God has greater purposes for immigration than short-term goals perceived by nations or particular immigrants themselves.

1. God is in charge of immigration.

Different nations have different rules about immigration. Nations make up these rules based on their perceived national needs and priorities. America, for instance, has been a very generous nation in terms of welcoming immigrants. It is truly a land of opportunity for immigrants. People from most nations of the world are allowed to immigrate to America within certain rules and quotas. They are allowed to become naturalized citizens through prescribed procedures. Many nations invite immigrants as laborers or skilled workers, but would never offer them citizenship or its full benefits. The United States gives naturalized citizens all the privileges that a native-born citizen enjoys, except the right to become president of the United States. This is certainly understandable.

I am a very grateful immigrant. This land has been very generous to me and my family. I have enjoyed freedom of conscience and freedom of movement within this vast land. In fact, crossing the border by car between Kerala state and Tamil Nadu state in my native country of India is an unpleasant experience, as everyone is required to stop and deal with the border police.

The United States Immigration and Naturalization Services (INS), now called United States Citizenship and Immigration Services (USCIS), governs US immigration. Since the late 1960s, family reunification has been the criterion by which preference is given to individuals wishing to immigrate to America. While some nations give priority to people with money and higher education, the United States has emphasized family relationships. A change in this way of looking at immigration is now being discussed for several reasons.

I believe the United States has the right to decide who comes in and who does not. In that sense, the USCIS has the legal power and should have the authority to control immigration. I have always obeyed the USCIS rules, even when they caused me to be long-suffering. However, I have come to realize that behind the power of the USCIS department moves the hand of God. The earth is the LORD's, says the Bible (Ps. 24:1). I am convinced that He decides who goes where. Even through our personal and corporate decisions about who goes where, I believe God is at work. Immigrants and natives need to keep this in mind as decisions are made.

2. God takes care of immigrants.

I see in the Bible how God took care of the immigrants of the past. Whether it was the prodigal son, who got employment at the pig farm, or Joseph, who found friends in prison, God took care of immigrants. I personally know many stories of current immigrants in terms of how God met their needs supernaturally. I can think of many people who were a blessing to me personally at different stages of my life as an immigrant during the last forty-five years. I hope this thought brings comfort to all immigrants.

I also see how God blesses the natives through the immigrants. The young Hebrew girl who witnessed to Naaman the leper about her healing God comes to mind (2 Kings 5:2–4).

3. God has greater purposes for immigration.

Immigrants may see only economic advantage or political safety in immigration. They may only see a better livelihood for their own families and loved ones. Nations may only see national objectives being met through immigration policies. I am convinced, however, that God accomplishes bigger and longer-lasting outcomes through immigration.

There are plenty of examples of this in the Bible. God wanted to bless the nations of the earth through Abraham's movement toward the Promised Land. He wanted to provide for Joseph's starving brothers by sending him ahead of them to Egypt. God wanted to save the world by sending His Son into the world, but before His arrival, a Moabite woman by the name of Ruth had to be moved to Palestine to become His great-great-great-great . . . grandmother.

I wonder what God is up to through current US immigration policies. There are some aspects of the situation that concern me. However, I am very optimistic about the number of highly educated historic Christians from India who have migrated to America in recent years—Christians from the land where the gospel of Jesus was first preached by Saint Thomas. A land where the good news could not be silenced for two thousand years!

Many of these immigrants are filled with the Holy Spirit. These are people who love the Lord Jesus Christ and value families. They represent two thousand years of Christian heritage, evangelization, and peaceful coexistence with other religions. They must be here at this hour for a reason bigger than globalization and economic advantage. God may have wanted them here precisely now, at this time in history. He may have wanted them to be role models of Christian family values and hope bearing. He may have wanted them to bear witness to the cross of Jesus Christ in an increasingly secularizing pluralistic nation and to expand the kingdom of God in these last days.

Christian immigrants are an untapped resource. I hope American churches will identify these cross-cultural disciples and change agents and empower them to reach the non-Christian immigrants in America and the billions of lost souls in their native lands.

48

THE WATER IN MY GARAGE: LOOKING BACK AT Y2K

*(*N*ote: On January 1, 2000, a worldwide catastrophe was expected due to anticipated global computer crashes caused by programming problems. This was called Y2K. The catastrophe never took place. This article, reflecting on the incident, was written during the first week of the new millennium.)*

This is the story of my Y2K preparedness back in 1999, and the lessons I learned from the Y2K nonevent. Computers were expected to crash on January 1, 2000, due to pre-programming issues, and to cause a great global catastrophe.

I heard the term *Y2K* for the first time in 1998 from my brother-in-law who is a minister. During 1999, I read several articles on the Y2K computer bug, but did not feel very concerned. However, toward the end of the year, the publicity became so intense that I began to pay more attention to the Y2K issue. I read about people who were stocking up food and buying guns to protect the food. I laughed at them, but when Christian

177

periodicals advised normal precautions, I felt that I should do something so that I would not feel irresponsible if any of the predictions were to come true.

I finally decided to buy enough bottled water and nonperishable foods to last through a long weekend of severely bad weather. I stored the bottled water in my garage. On December 31, 1999, we filled up our bathtub with water for use as nondrinking water and attended the watch night service. The Y2K computer crash was a nonevent. No major crisis took place. We kept our bathtub filled for two days and finally let the water go. The only result was that I was stuck with several large bottles of drinking water in my garage.

I was very disappointed that Americans were so frightened about the Y2K threat. I was especially concerned that American Christians were reportedly the most panicked group. I have asked myself why Christians allowed themselves to be more scared than the communists of Russia and China and the non-Christians of India. I still can't believe it. Is it true that we who talk about eternal life were the most fearful? Is it true that we who have our treasures laid up in heaven experienced the most anxiety? If these statements were true, then we have some soul searching to do.

I would like to believe that the reports were about nominal Christians, and not about born-again, Sprit-filled, holy-living, rapture-ready saints. We are to be a people of faith, hope, and love. Faith doesn't fear. Hope doesn't panic. And perfect love casts out fear (1 John 4:18). It should not be possible that we can be spooked to the point of buying guns to protect our dry beans from our hungry neighbors.

Then what about the water in my garage?

The drinking water in my garage tells me that I was greatly influenced by what I heard in the media. I was not immune to the constant talk about the impending doom. Although I did not go deep in debt to buy food and supplies, I did buy drinking water and enough food to last several days. Consider the fact that I grew up in an Indian parsonage, not always knowing where the next meal would come from. I should have known that God would supply all my needs according to His riches in glory (see Phil. 4:19). Instead, either the memory of past lack or fear of future hardship got the better of me. I should have allowed myself to be influenced more by the Word of God.

I do realize that one must be responsible and take reasonable precautions against predictable troubles. I may have done only that much. Nonetheless, these reflections are valid as they challenge us to get beyond our rationalizations and examine the depth of our commitment to Christ.

The drinking water in my garage tells me that my faith and hope must increase in the new millennium. I need to trust God more than I trust the media. God has promised to be our very present help in trouble, if trouble comes. Do I trust Him with all my strength?

I also need to anchor my life in biblical hope. Christians are a people of hope. We are called to be hope bearers. Despairing people should be able to look to us and see Christ in us, the hope of glory; instead they saw panicked Christians with other hopeless people in the store checkout lines. How is my hope? Do I put my hope in anything less than Jesus Christ?

The drinking water in my garage further reminds me that while the much-awaited Y2K doom did not happen, the much-ignored second coming of Christ will definitely happen. According to God's Word, "the Lord himself will come down from heaven . . . and the dead in Christ will rise first. After that, we who are still alive and are left will be caught up together with them in the clouds to meet the Lord in the air. And so we will be with the Lord forever" (1 Thess. 4:16–17).

Not only is the secular media silent about this; many modern preachers are also quiet on this subject. When was the last time you heard a sure message on the second coming of Christ? People enjoying material prosperity seldom want to hear about this topic. We should not let that stop us from declaring it. The truth is that God's Word will come to pass just as surely as man's predictions have failed this time.

Christian theology has always affirmed that Jesus Christ will come again. This is wonderful news to the church. God's people will be enjoying His presence. There is only one way to join the celebration: Simply put your whole life in the Lord's hand. Trust in the Lord Jesus Christ, and believe with all your heart that He died on the cross of Calvary for your sins. Your sins are forgiven when you believe in Him. You are given a new heart and life. He becomes your personal Lord and Savior and promises never to leave you or forsake you.

How can I buy drinking water and food to face a nonevent such as the Y2K breakdown and not be ready for the sure event of the coming of Christ? I have put my trust in Christ. The drinking water in my garage is persuading me to trust Him even more.

49

TRY TO SEE MILK AND HONEY, NOT GIANTS

Moses sent twelve spies to check out the land of promise. Only two of them came back with an encouraging report. The others said that they had seen giants in the land who made them feel like grasshoppers. They said this in spite of the fact that the evidence of "milk and honey" was right in front of them in the form of giant grapes brought back from the land (see Exod. 3:8; Num. 13:23).

Throughout the Bible we read of occasions when the people of God failed to see their potential blessings. They were so caught up in their circumstances that they could not see what God was preparing for them. This is well illustrated through the prophet's servant, who could see the human army lined up against God's people so clearly but could not see the heavenly host protecting them. The prophet prayed that the servant's eyes might be opened. They did open, and he saw God's great army (2 Kings 16).

Remember Philip, who told Jesus that even two hundred pennies' worth of bread could not feed the five-thousand-plus hungry people? He could only see the cost. He could only see their limitations. His spiritual eyes could not behold anything beyond the ordinary. Jesus was able to feed the multitude without a penny because there was a lad there with a little lunch and a lot of faith.

Lazarus's sister had the same issue. She could only report that her brother was dead and stinking! Jesus—the Resurrection and the Life—was standing right in front of her, but she could not see Him as the answer to her problem.

As you look into the future, what do you see: giants, or milk and honey? What are the giants you are focusing on? Are they financial problems or family situations? Are you preoccupied with worries and thoughts about your children's education and health issues? It is better to focus on the promises of God than to waste your energy worrying about the giants that may or may not exist.

The Bible speaks about three weapons we can use against any giants: the promises of God, the power of God, and the presence of God.

God's promises are true; He is a promise keeper. He made a promise to Abraham, and He kept His Word. The promises of God brought the people of Israel to the Promised Land. The promises of God defeated their enemies.

God's power saved His people from their enemies. The dividing of the Dead Sea and the sweet water of Marah testify to the power of God. He is the same yesterday, today, and forever. We must not be afraid of the enemy.

God promised His presence to Moses. In fact, Moses did not want to do anything until God promised His presence to him. God's presence was with His people in the desert through the pillar of cloud and the pillar of fire. His presence was in the tabernacle and the temple. The enemies of God scattered at His presence. Our God is an awesome God.

How about looking back and seeing God's provisions of the past? How about looking into God's Word to see the great promises? What about looking into God's face in prayer to see His mercies that are new every day? Lift up your head and behold His power and His presence; see the land of promise in this new millennium. Notice the giant grapes of God's current provisions and visualize the milk and honey of His promises. Let us trust God and His promises in the twenty-first century.

50

PRESERVING A SOUND MIND AS A DISCIPLE

The Bible assures us that God, through His Spirit, has given us (Spirit-led Christians) a sound mind (2 Tim. 1:7). Here are some biblical guidelines for preserving a sound mind.

Believe God Always

A Christian is to believe God always and in everything. He is never to question God's ability even when he cannot understand God's ways. God's grace is sufficient for the believer, always and everywhere. Faith in God and His promises will preserve a sound mind.

Have a Biblical Lifestyle

Life, according to the Bible, must include work and exercise, rest and play. The Bible encourages people to work to earn their living. Paul encouraged Christians to work "with their own hands" (Eph. 4:28 NIV). An idle mind is the devil's workshop.

Paul worked as a tentmaker and earned his living; he also supported others with his income (Acts 18:3; 20:34). Work is good, and so is needed rest. Jesus advised His disciples to come apart "into a desert place, and rest a while" (Mark 6:31 KJV). Overwork and fatigue are counterproductive, for "except the LORD build the house, they labour in vain that build it" (Ps. 127:1 KJV). Hence, take time for recreation. You will preserve a sound mind.

Have a Consistent Devotional Life

God's Word is meant to be a regular part of a Christian's diet. A Christian is to start each day with meditation and prayer. Keeping God's Word in our hearts all day long helps us to apply biblical principles to the many daily situations. God's great men—all of them—had a deep and consistent devotional life. David had a devotional life. He says in Psalm 63:1, "O God, thou art my God; early will I seek thee" (KJV). Daniel had a consistent devotional life (Dan. 6:10). A consistent devotional life preserves a sound mind.

Express Your Feelings

Many people are afraid to cry. Crying is understood by many as an expression of weakness, but the truth is contrary to this popular myth. Many great men have cried; Jesus himself wept before his disciples (John 11:35). Being able to release one's true feelings in this natural way is a blessing.

Both crying and laughing are part of healthy living. "A merry heart doeth good like a medicine," says the wise man (Prov. 17:22 KJV). Paul admonished the Roman believers, "Rejoice with them that do rejoice, and weep with them that weep" (Rom. 12:15 KJV). Good laughter is a gift from God to

His people. "Behold, God will not cast away a perfect man . . . till he fill thy mouth with laughing, and thy lips with rejoicing" (Job 8:20–21 KJV).

A good sense of humor is a great asset. I believe that Jesus had a beautiful and sacred sense of humor. Only a man with a great sense of humor could state the truth about the unbelieving rich man like this: "It is easier for a camel to go through the eye of a needle, than for a rich man to enter into the kingdom of God" (Matt. 19:24 KJV). The Bible shows us the serious side of Jesus' life, yet we see glimpses of many light moments. I do not believe Jesus wore a somber expression when he was with the little children who were brought to be blessed by Him.

Think On Positive Things

"With God all things are possible" (Matt, 19:26). "All things are possible to him that believeth" (Mark 9:23 KJV). A Christian must keep her thoughts positive, acknowledging God's power to work in her life: "If God be for us, who can be against us?" (Rom. 8:31 KJV). A Christian must avoid envy, jealousy, suspicion, and fear, also refusing to entertain feelings of revenge or self-pity. These thoughts destroy life. "Vengeance is mine; I will repay, saith the Lord. . . . Be not overcome of evil, but overcome evil with good" (Rom. 12:19, 21 KJV). Evil does exist, but a Christian can see beyond the evil.

We are to be loyal, kind, and generous. We are to be trusting and trustworthy. We must choose to see the good side of things. We must avoid gossip and keep good company.

Do Not Be Afraid to Love

Loving is trusting.

Loving is taking a chance.

Loving is giving.

Love God.

Love His Word.

Love His people.

With God's help, we are to love even those who persecute us (Matt. 5:44). A sound mind always accompanies a loving heart. The apostle John's final sermons are summarized in these words: "Beloved, let us love one another: for love is of God, and everyone that loveth is born of God, and knoweth God. He that loveth not knoweth not God; for God is love" (1 John 4:7– 8 KJV).

Worship God Regularly

A disciple of Jesus Christ must not misuse the Lord's day; on this day we must find ourselves in His house. It is a very good practice to locate the nearest Bible-believing church, even when visiting from out of town. A Christian must not waste time on excuses for not going to church. There is never a good excuse for failing to make the effort to worship God in fellowship with other Christians.

Jesus had the good custom of going to the house of God. "As his custom was, he went into the synagogue on the sabbath day" (Luke 4:16 KJV).

The apostle John spent time alone on the island of Patmos, banished there because of the gospel. But even in exile, he worshipped the Lord, alone, on the Lord's Day (Rev. 1:10). Worshipping God revitalizes the human spirit. A healthy spirit, a healthy mind, and a healthy body make a healthy, whole person.

51

LIVING LIKE HABAKKUK
IN THE AGE OF TERROR

It does not have the easiest or the fanciest name, but the Bible's book of Habakkuk contains a vital message for our time. How would you name our time? The age of globalization? The age of prosperity? The age of technology? All of these might be fitting names, but the fittest name is the age of terror.

I never thought we would live with the fear of terrorism in America, the land to which terrorized people from other nations have always run for safety. This is still the land of the free and the home of the brave, but we have been profoundly affected by the events of September 11, 2001, and the turmoil around the world since then. From New Delhi to New York, people are concerned about radical Islam and the threat it poses to free societies. Radical Islam is afraid of open societies and the free exchange of ideas. Democracy frightens radical Muslims.

An explanation of the causes of terrorism is way beyond the scope of this article, but there are those who believe that the current radical Islamic revolution is a cry of the hopeless masses for a reformation within Islam itself. Unfortunately, Islam may not be capable of reforming itself by the very nature of its theology. Had it not been for the sixteenth-century Reformation, Christianity and Western civilization may not have survived modern times as they did. One can only hope that Islam finds a release valve within its own ideology.

It would be grossly unfair to call all Muslims terrorists. There are Muslims who do not believe that a cartoonist should be killed for his offensive work or that a writer should be put to death for his unorthodox ideas. However, as long as they are not able to control their violent brethren or help them reform their theology or give them hope in some form or shape, Buddhist statues in Afghanistan as well as twin towers in New York City and commuter trains in Bombay, London, and Madrid are not the only things on the endangered list. Radical Islam breeds suicide bombers and spreads terror and fear among the world's citizens.

While Islamic terrorists and suicide bombers have ignited our fears, our own responses to them have not done much to reduce our anxieties. I am afraid that we may have inadvertently increased our own fears. In any case, from high school campuses to high places of society, fear has become a significant factor in our lives.

It is not difficult to frighten the masses. Look back to the way things were immediately after 9/11: We were eerily silent. We looked for clues to reduce our fears and, in turn, managed to increase our fright. Whether it is the Y2K scare or post-9/11 incidents, we have learned to be more afraid than usual. Fear makes us become suspicious of people, especially those unlike us.

Fear alienates. It affects mental health and spiritual well-being. Long-term fear will take its toll on us. How do we avoid this? How shall we live in a fearless way in these fearful times? Are there examples of such a way of living?

This is where Habakkuk can help us. He was a believer who lived in Jerusalem six hundred years before Christ. It is hard to believe that terrorism existed before our time; but the fact is that terrorists and terrorism are not new on planet Earth. Only their methods have been updated. Habakkuk was an eyewitness to fear and terror.

Assyria was the ruling empire during his time. It was going down fast. Egypt and Babylon were fighting to take the place left by Assyria. They each wanted to be the next superpower. These were two powerful cultures of their day. Babylon won this fight in 605 BC. Nebuchadnezzar became the ruler of the entire civilized world at that time. He was the most powerful man on earth. Just seven years before, in 612 BC, Nineveh had fallen. Habakkuk lived and wrote during this turbulent period. His book describes a crisis time.

Sounds familiar? Fall of an empire! Remember the Soviet Union and the fall of the Berlin Wall? Fight for superpower status! China wants to be the next superpower. The Europeans would like to claim that title too. Clash of civilizations between Babylonians and Egyptians! We are familiar with this too now. Listen to Habakkuk. He was an eyewitness to injustices and conflicts. He sounds like a contemporary embedded reporter!

Habakkuk asks, "How long, LORD, must I call for help, but you do not listen? Or cry out to you, 'Violence!' but you do not save? Why do you make me look at injustice? Why do you tolerate wrongdoing? Destruction and violence are before me; there is strife, and conflict abounds" (Hab. 1:2–3 NIV).

Habakkuk is so fed up that he is questioning God. *How can you stand it, God? How can you allow this?* "Your eyes are too pure to look on evil; you cannot tolerate wrongdoing. Why then do you tolerate the treacherous? Why are you silent while the wicked swallow up those more righteous than themselves?" (v. 13 NIV). Habakkuk describes the anarchy of his day: "The law is paralyzed, and justice never prevails. The wicked hem in the righteous, so that justice is perverted" (v. 4 NIV).

Habakkuk is very concerned about the political, social, and spiritual situation in which he finds himself. His context is frightening. Idolatry seems to be pervading his society. He is not a happy camper at this point.

"Of what value is an idol carved by a craftsman? Or an image that teaches lies? For the one who makes it trusts in his own creation; he makes idols that cannot speak. Woe to him who says to wood, 'Come to life!' Or to lifeless stone, 'Wake up!' Can it give guidance? It is covered with gold and silver; there is no breath in it" (Hab. 2:18–19 NIV).

His situation is dire, but to his utter despair, Habakkuk is expecting conditions to get worse. He is anticipating a worse calamity. Listen to him: "I heard and my heart pounded, my lips quivered at the sound; decay crept into my bones, and my legs trembled. Yet I will wait patiently for the day of calamity to come on the nation invading us" (Hab. 3:16 NIV).

Habakkuk is a man of strong faith, but he is overwhelmed. He has some serious questions for God. His questions and God's answers to them help us discover the way we ought to live at such a time as ours.

Asking questions is not a sign of lack of faith. God is not offended by the questions of His children. Habakkuk's questions can be divided into two general categories: *Why?* and *How long?* God does not answer Habakkuk with neat answers, but He does tell Habakkuk how to live at such a time as his. So, how does a believer live in violent times?

God Is in Charge

God's first response to Habakkuk is that He is in charge of the world. Often, we live as if someone other than God is in charge of the world and its history. God wants Habakkuk to learn that "the earth is the LORD's, and everything in it, the world, and all who live in it" (Ps. 24:1 NIV). He wants him to conclude: "The LORD is in his holy temple: let all the earth keep silence before him" (Hab. 2:20 KJV). This is an important truth for Habakkuk to contemplate.

The lesson from Genesis to Revelation is that God is involved in His creation. He is in charge even when bad things seem to be happening. He is in charge when unpleasant things happen seemingly out of control. God is in charge. This is true at all times. There is no time when God is not in charge.

It is natural for us to wonder about God's role in the world at times when world events are overwhelming. We want to make sense of the chaos around us. When things do not make any sense, we are prone to wonder about God's place in the world. This is especially true when we observe the suffering of the innocent. Why should a good God allow such bad things to happen? The fact is, we do not know the answer to that question fully yet, but we should not forget that most of the things that cause us to rail against God are created or done by man—God's creation entrusted with a free will!

God is in charge of life and everything in it. We can be sure that God's purposes are being accomplished in this world. We need to remember this in times of violence—just as Habakkuk did. We need to remember this when fear grips our souls. We also have to remember that the God who is in charge of the world is a good God. His goodness has no end. He is love. A good response to God on our part is to be like the psalmist and say, "Give thanks to the LORD, for he is good; his love endures forever" (Ps. 107:1 NIV).

Idols are not in charge of the world. God is. God speaks. God is alive. He guides His people. He is in charge.

This means that the Taliban is not in charge. Al-Qaeda is not in charge. Jihadists are not in charge. Hamas is not in charge. Hezbollah is not in charge. In fact, even the United Nations is not in charge of the world. God is. Why should we live in fear?

Live by Faith

The second answer Habakkuk receives is this: "The righteous will live by his faith" (Hab. 2:4 NASB). We are constantly tempted to live by sight, but living by sight can be a scary experience. Faith sees the invisible, believes the incredible, and accomplishes the impossible. To live without fear, we must learn to live by faith. We need to live by faith in peacetime. We must also learn to live by faith during times of conflict.

Living by faith requires us to trust God and depend on Him. This is not easy for modern people. We want to depend on ourselves. We want to be secure and self-sufficient. But Habakkuk says that there is no such thing as living by sight without fear.

The Bible contains the story of those who lived by faith and instructions on how to live like them. Hebrews 11 is an example of this. Enoch, Abraham, Isaac, Jacob, Joseph, and Moses are among those who were commended for their faith. There are also countless individuals whose names are not given, but their life of faith is described in detail. They through faith conquered kingdoms, administered justice, and gained what was promised; who shut the mouths of lions, quenched the fury of the flames, and escaped the edge of the sword; whose weakness was turned to strength; and who became powerful in battle and routed foreign armies. Women received back their dead, raised to life again. There were others who were tortured, refusing to be released so that they might gain an even better resurrection. Some faced jeers and flogging, and even chains and imprisonment. They were put to death by stoning; they were sawed in two; they were killed by the sword. They went about in sheepskins and goatskins, destitute, persecuted and mistreated— the world was not worthy of them. They wandered in deserts and mountains, living in caves and in holes in the ground. (Heb. 11:33–38 NIV)

A life of faith is a life of triumphs and trials. On one hand, it enables one to conquer kingdoms and receive back the dead. On the other hand, it may cause one to wander in deserts, mountains, caves, and holes in the ground or cause one to be sawed in two or stoned to death! It is clear that faith is not for wimps. Faith requires strength and courage.

Living without fear requires living by faith. This day and age require such living.

Live by Hope

Habakkuk learns to live by hope. In fact, in the midst of utter chaos, he begins to practice hope by declaring that "the earth will be filled with the knowledge of the glory of the LORD, as the waters cover the sea" (Hab. 2:14). Imagine! Violence surrounds the prophet. Injustices abound. The wicked are flourishing. The innocent are suffering. But the prophet is a man of hope who sees by faith a time in the future when the knowledge of the glory of the Lord will fill the earth. It will be deep and wide and vast as the ocean.

Crisis times call us to be hope bearers. Christians are called to be hope carriers because we carry Christ in us. We know that "God has chosen to make known among the Gentiles the glorious riches of this mystery, which is Christ in you, the hope of glory" (Col. 1:27 NIV).

We live in a world of hopeless people. Hopelessness is at the root of violence in many parts of the world today. The Middle East crisis, especially, needs to be examined in this regard. Hopelessness creates suicide bombers. Bullets won't stop them.

But hope will.

52

WHAT WILL YOUR TOMBSTONE SAY?

It was a typical day in my Pastoral Care class at Oral Roberts University. "Death and dying" was the topic of the day. Normally, during this session I would cover a biblical understanding of death, Elisabeth Kübler-Ross's research on stages of grief, and various issues of ministry to the bereaved that future pastors need to know. Since death is a difficult topic to cover, I decided to start the class with an icebreaker. I asked the students to think about their future deaths. I gave them some questions to think about: When will you die? What type of death will it be? What type of death do you prefer? What type of funeral service would you want?

The class became very quiet as students began to think of their own mortality. No one was speaking. Finally, I asked them to take a piece of paper and write on it their own epitaphs—the words they would want on their tombstones. There was absolute silence in the class by then. The tension was high. Everyone was looking down and writing. No one spoke.

One student finally raised his hand and said he was ready to share his epitaph with the class. I asked him to read it to us. He read, "'I told you I was sick!' That's what will be on my tombstone." The whole class laughed out loud. The tension was broken, and students began to share what they really wanted on their tombstones.

"He was a good father," one said. "He was a man of God," another one said. "She really cared," another one read. "She loved all," another one said. A sober discussion about life, death, discipleship, and ministry followed.

It is amazing how our words and actions change when we become aware of our own mortality. Once we recognize that after everything is said and done, we are mortal beings saved by the grace of God and eternally at His mercy, we begin to think and act differently. People who have encountered a life-threatening situation often testify to this. They report that they have a new appreciation for life. Their priorities change. The nature of their relationships also changes.

It is almost impossible to think of one's mortality during one's teenage years. Teenagers often think of themselves as invincible. Most people think of their mortality only when they reach middle age. However, Christians of all ages are to live as people who have encountered their own mortality because they share this unique testimony with Saint Paul: "I am crucified with Christ: nevertheless, I live" (Gal. 2:20 KJV).

A Christian is dead to sin, self, and the world. This is the ultimate acceptance of one's mortality at any age. However, the Christian is also very much alive at the same time because we have not only been buried with Christ, but also have been raised with Him to live in newness of life (Rom. 6:4).

The Christian faith has the cross of Jesus at its center. The cross is a symbol of self-denial and death. The Christian cross is also an empty cross that points the way to an empty tomb and an upper room. We are to live our lives as crucified people who have tasted the power of Christ's resurrection. We have already been seated in heavenly places (Eph. 2:6). In other words, we are to live our lives in the fullness of the Spirit and in the awareness of the life, death, and resurrection of Jesus Christ.

We live, however, in a culture of materialism, violence, and self-centeredness. Even a church can become a place of materialism, arrogance, and self-promotion. We must guard against anything that could drown out the gentle whisper of the Holy Spirit reminding us of the eternity in our souls.

What is the Holy Spirit saying to us today? I believe the Spirit is saying that we must be concerned about the lostness of our world. We must be concerned about the pains of the world, because God is still concerned about His lost and hurting world.

George Barna has reminded us that we are not called just to *go* to church, but to *be* the church.[25] Oral Roberts expressed the same idea long ago when he said, "We must go into every person's world"—some as ministers and others as disciples with their own professions. We must share the good news of Jesus Christ with our dying world. It must be shared by all Christians—men and women empowered by the Holy Spirit.

Credentials are not as important as calling is to do this work. Competence is not as important as character. What is required is self-giving, not self-promotion. What is really needed is a crucified heart filled with the Holy Spirit. Only someone who has faced his own mortality and embraced eternity can give his

---

25 George Barna, *Revolution* (Carol Stream, IL: Tyndale: 2006), 39.

life away. Maybe the epitaph for such a person will read, "He gave his life away—gladly! And saved it."

What will your tombstone say?

www.thomsonkmathew.com

OTHER BOOKS BY
THOMSON K. MATHEW

Spiritual Identity and Spirit-Empowered Life:
Discover Your Identity in God's Family,
Purpose in God's Call, and Power in God's Spirit

"Jesus I know, and Paul I know about, but who are you?" The Bible describes the experience of a group of religious people who could not answer this question and as a result suffered serious trauma (Acts 19:15 NIV). How would you answer this question? Living as a whole person in this broken world requires being able to answer this question correctly and having a strong spiritual identity. This volume, written by a pastor, chaplain, and seminary professor, presents spiritual identity in 3-D and helps you discover and affirm your true identity in God, beyond your national, racial, ethnic, and all other identities.

Reading this book and prayerfully reflecting on its content privately or in a group setting will help you establish your spiritual identity by discovering your primary identity in God's family, your purpose in God's call, and the power to fulfill your destiny in God's Spirit.

Written in easy-to-read language with inspiring stories, this book contains biblically sound, theologically balanced, and spiritually impacting instruction. Read, reflect, and be transformed.

Spirit-Led Ministry in the Twenty-First Century, Revised and Updated Edition:
Empowered Preaching, Teaching, Healing, and Leadership

This book is a comprehensive guide to competent Spirit-led ministry in the twenty-first century. Written from a Pentecostal/charismatic perspective, it focuses on four important aspects of effective ministry: preaching, teaching, healing, and leading. Beginning with biblical definitions of ministry, the book describes the challenges presented by the twenty-first century in light of the long history of Christian ministry, and it offers biblically sound advice to address these challenges. The role of the Holy Spirit in ministry is examined in detail. The bulk of the book is devoted to the theory (theology) and practice of competent, Spirit-led ministry. This book is a call to excellence in ministry, as well as a guide to empowered preaching, teaching, healing, and leading.

Ministry Between Miracles:
Caring for Hurting People in the Power of the Holy Spirit

This book by an experienced pastor and hospital chaplain will help you:
- develop your caring skills
- bring healing to people in pain

- enhance your God-given gifts for caregiving
- experience new success in helping people become whole.

In *Ministry Between Miracles*, Spirit-filled pastors, counselors, and lay caregivers will find fresh perspectives on:
- biblical concepts of pastoral care
- avoiding dangerous mistakes
- how to move in the power of the Holy Spirit to bring new spiritual freedom.

We must practice Spirit-led caregiving with maximum integrity. We must prepare ourselves through proper training to offer skillful caregiving, and then surrender those skills to the Master.

www.thomsonkmathew.com